MACMILLAN MASTER GUIDES
THE WINTER'S TALE
BY WILLIAM SHAKESPEARE

DIANA DEVLIN

with an introduction by
HAROLD BROOKS

MACMILLAN

First published 1985 by
THE MACMILLAN PRESS LTD
Houndmills, Basingstoke, Hampshire RG21 2XS
and London
Companies and representatives
throughout the world

ISBN 0–333–38571–3

A catalogue record for this book is available
from the British Library.

Reprinted 1994

Printed in China

CONTENTS

General editor's preface   vi

Acknowledgements   vii

An introduction to the study of Shakespeare's plays   viii

1 Shakespeare and   1.1 William Shakespeare   1
  his Theatre   1.2 Shakespeare's Theatre   2
                       1.3 Staging *The Winter's Tale*   3
                       1.4 *The Winter's Tale* and con-
                           temporary drama   4

2 Summaries and critical   2.1 Summary of the play   6
  commentary   2.2 Chapter summaries and
                               commentary   7

3 Themes   3.1 Leontes's jealousy and its
                           consequences   48
                       3.2 Loss and discovery - Perdita's
                           double identity   49
                       3.3 The resurrection of Hermione   50
                       3.4 Time and the seasons   51
                       3.5 The Oracle and its fulfilment   51
                       3.6 Human life as a drama -
                           an overview of the play   52

4 Technical features   4.1 Language   54
                       4.2 Plot and structure   57
                       4.3 Characterisation   59
                       4.4 Stagecraft   66
                       4.5 Style   68

5 Critical reception and   72
  stage history

6 Specimen passage   75

Revision questions   78

Appendix: Shakespeare's Theatre   79

Further reading   83

GENERAL EDITOR'S PREFACE

The aim of the Macmillan Master Guides is to help you to appreciate the book you are studying by providing information about it and by suggesting ways of reading and thinking about it which will lead to a fuller understanding. The section on the writer's life and background has been designed to illustrate those aspects of the writer's life which have influenced the work, and to place it in its personal and literary context. The summaries and critical commentary are of special importance in that each brief summary of the action is followed by an examination of the significant critical points. The space which might have been given to repetitive explanatory notes has been devoted to a detailed analysis of the kind of passage which might confront you in an examination. Literary criticism is concerned with both the broader aspects of the work being studied and with its detail. The ideas which meet us in reading a great work of literature, and their relevance to us today, are an essential part of our study, and our Guides look at the thought of their subject in some detail. But just as essential is the craft with which the writer has constructed his work of art, and this is considered under several technical headings - characterisation, language, style and stagecraft.

The authors of these Guides are all teachers and writers of wide experience, and they have chosen to write about books they admire and know well in the belief that they can communicate their admiration to you. But you yourself must read and know intimately the book you are studying. No one can do that for you. You should see this book as a lamppost. Use it to shed light, not to lean against. If you know your text and know what it is saying about life, and how it says it, then you will enjoy it, and there is no better way of passing an examination in literature.

JAMES GIBSON

ACKNOWLEDGEMENTS

All quotations are from *The Winter's Tale* edited by Christopher Parry, *The Macmillan Shakespeare* (Macmillan Education, 1982). Cover illustration: *The Shepherd's Cot* from *The Winter's Tale*, Act IV, Scene 3, by William Hamilton. Courtesy of the Governors of the Royal Shakespeare Theatre, Stratford-upon-Avon. The drawing of the Globe Theatre is by courtesy of Alec Pearson.

AN INTRODUCTION TO THE STUDY OF SHAKESPEARE'S PLAYS

A play as a work of art exists to the full only when performed. It must hold the audience's attention throughout the performance, and, unlike a novel, it can't be put down and taken up again. It is important to experience the play as if you are seeing it on the stage for the first time, and you should begin by reading it straight through. Shakespeare builds a play in dramatic units which may be divided into smaller subdivisions, or episodes, marked off by exits and entrances and lasting as long as the same actors are on the stage. Study it unit by unit.

The first unit provides the exposition which is designed to put the audience into the picture. In the second unit we see the forward movement of the play as one situation changes into another. The last unit in a tragedy or a tragical play will bring the catastrophe and in comedy – and some of the history plays – an unravelling of the complications, what is called a *dénouement*.

The onward movement of the play from start to finish is its progressive structure. We see the chain of cause and effect (the plot) and the progressive revelation and development of character. The people, their characters and their motives drive the plot forward in a series of scenes which are carefully planned to give variety of pace and excitement. We notice fast-moving and slower-moving episodes, tension mounting and slackening, and alternate fear and hope for the characters we favour. Full-stage scenes, such as stately councils and processions or turbulent mobs, contrast with scenes of small groups or even single speakers. Each of the scenes presents a deed or event which changes the situation. In performance, entrances and exits and stage actions are physical facts, with more impact than on the page. That impact Shakespeare relied upon, and we must restore it by an effort of the imagination.

Shakespeare's language is just as diverse. Quickfire dialogue is followed by long speeches, and verse changes to prose. There is a wide range of speech – formal, colloquial, dialect, 'Mummerset' and the broken English of foreigners, for example. Songs, instrumental music, and the noise of battle, revelry and tempest, all extend the range of dramatic expression. The dramatic use of language is enhanced by skilful stagecraft, by costumes, by properties such as beds, swords and Yorick's skull, by such stage business as kneeling, embracing and giving money, and by use of such features of the stage structure as the balcony and the trapdoor.

By these means Shakespeare's people are brought vividly to life and cleverly individualised. But though they have much to tell us about human nature, we must never forget that they are characters in a play, not in real life. And remember, they exist to enact the play, not the play to portray *them*.

Shakespeare groups his characters so that they form a pattern, and it is useful to draw a diagram showing this. Sometimes a linking character has dealings with each group. The pattern of persons belongs to the symmetric structure of the play, and its dramatic unity is reinforced and enriched by a pattern of resemblances and contrasts: for instance, between characters, scenes, recurrent kinds of imagery, and words. It is not enough just to notice a feature that belongs to the symmetric structure, you should ask what its relevance is to the play as a whole and to the play's ideas.

These ideas and the dramatising of them in a central theme, or several related to each other, are a principal source of the dramatic unity. In order to see what themes are present and important, look, as before, for pattern. Observe the place in it of the leading character. In tragedy this will be the protagonist, in comedy heroes and heroines, together with those in conflict or contrast with them. In *I Henry IV*, Prince Hal is being educated for kingship and has a correct estimate of honour, while Falstaff despises honour, and Hotspur makes an idol of it. Pick out the episodes of great intensity as, for example, in *King Lear* where the theme of spiritual blindness is objectified in the blinding of Gloucester, and, similarly, note the emphases given by dramatic poetry as in Prospero's 'Our revels now are ended. . .' or unforgettable utterances such as Lear's. 'Is there any cause in Nature that makes these hard hearts?' Striking stage-pictures such as that of Hamlet behind the King at prayer will point to leading themes, as will all the parallels and recurrences, including those of phrase and imagery. See whether, in the play you are studying, themes known to be favourites with Shakespeare are prominent, themes such as those of order and disorder, relationships disrupted by mistakes about identity, and appearance and reality. The latter were bound to fascinate Shakespeare whose theatrical art worked by means of illusions which pointed beyond the surface of actual life to underlying truths. In looking at themes beware of attempts to make the play fit some orthodoxy a critic believes in – Freudian perhaps, or Marxist, or dogmatic Christian theology – and remember that its ideas, though they often have a bearing on ours, are Elizabethan.

Some of Shakespeare's greatness lies in the good parts he wrote for the actors. In his demands upon them, and the opportunities he provided, he bore their professional skills in mind and made use of their physical prowess, relished by a public accustomed to judge fencing and wrestling as expertly as we today judge football and tennis. As a member of the professional group of players called the Chamberlain's Men he knew each actor he was writing for. To play his women he had highly-trained boys. As paired heroines they were often contrasted, short with tall, for example, or one vivacious and enterprising, the other more conventionally feminine.

Richard Burbage, the company's leading man, was famous as a great tragic actor, and he took leading roles in seven of Shakespeare's *tragedies*. Though each of the seven has its own distinctiveness, we shall find at the centre of all of them a tragic protagonist possessing tragic greatness, not just one 'tragic flaw' but a tragic vulnerability. He will have a character which makes him unfit to cope with the tragic situations confronting him, so that his tragic errors bring down upon him tragic suffering and finally a tragic catastrophe. Normally, both the suffering and the catastrophe are far worse than he can be said to deserve, and others are engulfed in them who deserve such a fate less or not at all. Tragic terror is aroused in us because, though exceptional, he is sufficiently near to normal humankind for his fate to remind us of what can happen to human beings like ourselves and because we see in it a combination of inexorable law and painful mystery. We recognise the principle of cause and effect where in a tragic world errors return upon those who make them, but we are also aware of the tragic disproportion between cause and effect. In a tragic world you may kick a stone and start an avalanche which will destroy you and others with you. Tragic pity is aroused in us by this disproportionate suffering, and also by all the kinds of suffering undergone by every character who has won our imaginative sympathy. Imaginative sympathy is wider than moral approval, and is felt even if suffering does seem a just and logical outcome. In addition to pity and terror we have a sense of tragic waste because catastrophe has affected so much that was great and fine. Yet we feel also a tragic exaltation. To our grief the men and women who represented those values have been destroyed, but the values themselves have been shown not to depend upon success, nor upon immunity from the worst of tragic suffering and disaster.

Comedies have been of two main kinds, or cross-bred from the two. In critical comedies the governing aim is to bring out the absurdity or irrationality of follies and abuses, and make us laugh at them. Shakespeare's comedies often do this, but most of them belong primarily to the other kind – romantic comedy. Part of the romantic appeal is to our liking for suspense; they are dramas of averted threat, beginning in trouble and ending in joy. They appeal to the romantic senses of adventure and of wonder, and to complain that they are improbable is silly because the improbability, the marvellousness, is part of the pleasure. They dramatise stories of romantic love, accompanied by love doctrine – ideas and ideals of love. But they are plays in two tones, they are comic as well as romantic. There is often something to laugh at even in the love stories of the nobility and gentry, and just as there is high comedy in such incidents as the cross-purposes of the young Athenians in the wood, and Rosalind as 'Ganymede' teasing Orlando, there is always broad comedy for characters of lower rank. Even where one of the sub-plots has no effect on the main plot, it may take up a topic from it and present it in a more comic way.

What is there in the play to make us laugh or smile? We can distinguish many kinds of comedy it may employ. *Language* can amuse by its wit, or by absurdity, as in Bottom's malapropisms. Feste's nonsense-phrases, so fatuously admired by Sir Andrew, are deliberate, while his catechising of Olivia is clown-routine. Ass-headed Bottom embraced by the Fairy Queen is a *comic spectacle* combining costume and stage-business. His wanting to play every part is *comedy of character*. Phebe disdaining Silvius and in love with 'Ganymede', or Malvolio treating Olivia as though she had written him a love-letter is *comedy of situation;* the situation is laughably different from what Phebe or Malvolio supposes. A comic let-down or anticlimax can be devastating, as we see when Aragon, sure that he deserves Portia, chooses the silver casket only to find the portrait not of her but of a 'blinking idiot'. By *slapstick, caricature* or sheer *ridiculousness of situation*, comedy can be exaggerated into farce, which Shakespeare knows how to use on occasion. At the opposite extreme, before he averts the threat, he can carry it to the brink of tragedy, but always under control.

Dramatic irony is the result of a character or the audience anticipating an outcome which, comically or tragically, turns out very differently. Sometimes *we* foresee that it will. The speaker never foresees how ironical, looking back, the words or expectations will appear. When she says, 'A little water clears us of this deed' Lady Macbeth has no prevision of her sleep-walking words, 'Will these hands ne'er be clean?' There is irony in the way in which in all Shakespeare's tragic plays except *Richard II* comedy is found in the very heart of the tragedy. The Porter scene in *Macbeth* comes straight after Duncan's murder. In *Hamlet* and *Antony and Cleopatra*. comic episodes lead into the catastrophe: the rustic Countryman brings Cleopatra the means of death, and the satirised Osric departs with Hamlet's assent to the fatal fencing match. The Porter, the Countryman and Osric are not mere 'comic relief', they contrast with the tragedy in a way that adds something to it, and affects our response.

A sense of the comic and the tragic is common ground between Shakespeare and his audience. Understandings shared with the audience are necessary to all drama. They include conventions, i.e. assumptions, contrary to what factual realism would demand, which the audience silently agrees to accept. It is, after all, by a convention, what Coleridge called a 'willing suspension of disbelief', that an actor is accepted as Hamlet. We should let a play teach us the conventions it depends on. Shakespeare's conventions allow him to take a good many liberties, and he never troubles about inconsistencies that wouldn't trouble an audience. What matters to the dramatist is the effect he creates. So long as we are responding as he would wish, Shakespeare would not care whether we could say by what means he has made us do so. But to appreciate his skill, and get a fuller understanding of his play, we have to distinguish these means, and find terms to describe them.

If you approach the Shakespeare play you are studying bearing in mind what is said to you here, then you will respond to it more fully than before. Yet like all works of artistic genius, Shakespeare's can only be analysed so far. His drama and its poetry will always have about them something 'which into words no critic can digest'.

HAROLD BROOKS

1 SHAKESPEARE AND HIS THEATRE

1.1 WILLIAM SHAKESPEARE

William Shakespeare was born in 1564 – during the reign of Queen Elizabeth I – in Stratford-upon-Avon in Warwickshire, where he spent his boyhood, married Anne Hathaway and produced three children. He came to London as a young man and, by 1592, had established a career as a dramatist and an actor. He joined a theatre company called the Lord Chamberlain's Men, who played at public theatres and at Court. In 1599, with other members of the company, he became a shareholder of the Globe, a newly-built theatre on Bankside in Southwark. When Queen Elizabeth died in 1603, King James I succeeded to the throne and took over the patronage of Shakespeare's company. The King's Men, as they were now called, were the foremost company of the period, and were often asked to perform at Court. In 1608 they assumed the lease of the Blackfriars, a small indoor theatre, which they used as their winter base. In 1611, Shakespeare bought a house back home in Stratford but his plays continued to be performed in London. He died in Stratford on 23 April, 1616.

The first collection of Shakespeare's plays was published in 1623. Over a period of about twenty years he wrote something like thirty-seven plays. There were many other popular playwrights of the time. Plays of the period are often still performed, but none has achieved the fame and popularity of Shakespeare, whose plays continue to delight and inspire audiences, readers and scholars throughout the world.

Some people have wondered if such a man as Shakespeare could have written the great plays attributed to him. Shakespeare probably went to school, where he would have received a good classical education, especially in Latin. Another source of education might have been the Church, which he would have attended regularly, but he was not as highly educated as many of his contemporaries. He did not go to university, and there is no evidence that he travelled or received any other cultural input other than was available in London. However the mystery of his greatness would not be solved by finding new facts about the man. He was writing at a time when there were many individuals and forces working to encourage good drama. The circumstances in which he wrote are the only evidence we have to explain the special quality of his work.

1.2 SHAKESPEARE'S THEATRE

Before the sixteenth century there was very little professional theatre in England. Plays were performed as part of religious and seasonal festivals, and as royal, aristocratic or civil entertainment. Professional entertainers such as minstrels toured the country or attached themselves to rich households. By Shakespeare's time, however, several companies had been formed under the patronage of noblemen to perform plays in halls, in yards and whatever other convenient places offered themselves. In 1576, the first purpose-built theatre in England was erected. It was in London, north-east of the city walls and built by James Burbage, whose son Richard became the leading actor in Shakespeare's company. The Theatre, known simply by that name, was pulled down in 1599 and re-erected as the Globe on Bankside, south of the river. By that time there were three other public theatres, and by the time Shakespeare died, two more, as well as several indoor theatres and conversions.

The professional companies had many problems to contend with, including religious and political opposition and outbreaks of the plague, but the Court, first under Queen Elizabeth, then under King James, encouraged the theatre and it became a very popular form of entertainment, drawing its audiences from all classes of society. During this period London was swiftly established as the important theatre centre which it has remained almost ever since. Shakespeare was attached to a prosperous company who performed everything he wrote as soon as the words were on paper. He was closely involved in the presentation, writing for actors whose talents he knew.

The Globe is described in detail on page 79. Performances there took place in the afternoon, lit by natural daylight. Audiences were often noisy and restless, but good actors telling a powerful story could hold them spellbound.

From 1609 the Blackfriars playhouse provided the King's Men with a theatre for the winter months. A very different kind of building from the Globe, the Blackfriars had several similar stage features. It was an indoor theatre, converted from a Great Hall 100 feet long and 46 feet wide. The raised stage was positioned about two-thirds of the way down the hall with the tiring house (the actors' dressing room) behind. The whole audience was seated, either in rows at floor level (or 'pit') or in the galleries or boxes that lined the long sides and end of the chamber. The theatre held about 700 people, many fewer than the Globe, yet the proportion and shape meant that the most distant spectators were much further from the stage than anyone at the Globe.

Theatre-going at Blackfriars was much more sophisticated than at the Globe. Performances took place at night and were lit by candles. Music was played between the Acts. Minimum admission was sixpence, six times the price of the cheapest entry to the Globe. The small audience was less rowdy, perhaps more discerning, but not necessarily more appreciative than at the Globe.

Entertainments at Court were lavishly presented, organised by the Master of the Revels to match the richness and elegance of the noble audience. King James had the Banqueting Hall rebuilt early in his reign. The basic shape was like the indoor theatres with the stage near one end of the hall, with rows and tiers of seats for the spectators. There were elegant classical columns at the sides and the King was placed on a throne of state at the end of the room, facing the stage. The scenery and costumes for court entertainments were resplendent, especially for the 'masques' which were spectacular presentations including music and dancing. For some masques a curtain was dropped in front of the scenery to conceal it until the piece began. Sometimes an arch was constructed in front of the stage, or part of it. This arch, called the proscenium, framed the stage picture. It allowed more complicated scenic effects to be achieved, and scenes to be changed out of sight of the audience.

1.3 STAGING *THE WINTER'S TALE*

The first recorded performance of *The Winter's Tale* was on 15 May, 1611 at the Globe. It was probably written earlier that year and may well have been performed at the Blackfriars as well as at the Globe. There are records of other performances during Shakespeare's lifetime, of special interest being a performance at Whitehall in February 1613, as part of the marriage celebrations of Princess Elizabeth, the King's daughter, to Prince Frederick, the Elector Palatine of the Rhine. Interestingly, she was to reign for a brief time as Queen of Bohemia, and would be known as the Winter Queen.

No details survive about the presentation of the play but the stage conventions at the Globe, the Blackfriars and the Banqueting Hall offer some indications. Very few props or scenery are required in the play. The

action would have been continuous, unless there was music provided
between the Acts at the Blackfriars. Music is called for in the pastoral
scene and also when the statue comes to life. The musicians were probably
placed in the balcony of the tiring house 'façade'. All the entrances and
exits were through the doorways there too. Sometimes these doorways
were covered with a curtain or hanging, which could be drawn back to
reveal a scene behind, either at floor level or on a small platform, which
could even be pushed on to the main stage. We can imagine the 'statue'
of Hermione posed behind a curtain in just such a way, looking as if she
was part of the decoration when the curtain was pulled back. In the flick-
ering candlelight of an indoor theatre this scene was probably even more
effective than in the daylight of the Globe playhouse, especially with a
smaller, more privileged audience. There were probably special effects
for the storm scene, and it has been suggested that the 'bear' might have
been a real one, kept for the bear-baiting which took place near the Globe.
Costumes were contemporary, with some 'classical' additions. They would
have been lavish, especially for the Court performance. Probably even the
pastoral scene was costumed artistically rather than realistically; and in
all likelihood the music and dancing were performed with the skill and
showmanship developed for court masques, rather than an imitation of
folk festivals.

Rehearsals were minimal, several new plays being presented every
month. The actors (there were no actresses) had to study quickly and
communicate effectively to the large and often unruly audience at the
Globe, as well as to the select gatherings at the Court. The one thing that
these audiences had in common which modern audiences lack was a
lively receptivity to the spoken word.

1.4 *THE WINTER'S TALE* AND THE CONTEMPORARY DRAMA

Shakespeare wrote *The Winter's Tale* near the end of his career. He had
already written many comedies, histories, and tragedies, following such
writers as Christopher Marlowe, George Peele, John Lyly and Robert Greene.
His last plays contained elements of comedy, tragedy and history, and he
developed them as romances combining sadness and joy, which was the
style made popular in the Jacobean theatre by such writers as Francis
Beaumont and John Fletcher. He was also influenced by the masque,
which the designer Inigo Jones was developing as court entertainment.

Although Shakespeare often shows men and women struggling with
their understanding of divine forces, he did not write openly religious
plays. The main reason for this was that such plays were forbidden.
Christianity was the accepted and enforced religion of his society, but

the Christian Church had recently split into Roman Catholic and the Protestant. Under Queen Elizabeth and King James, England was Protestant. There was much controversy, so the government kept strict control over religious practice and censored religious drama. However, Shakespeare's plays were strongly influenced by the religious drama of the generations that preceded his and *The Winter's Tale* has often been interpreted as a Christian allegory.

During Shakespeare's time, the image of the theatre itself stimulated exciting thoughts about the human condition. The motto of the Globe playhouse was *'Totus mundus agit histrionem'*, which loosely translates into Shakespeare's own line, 'All the world's a stage'. In *Hamlet* he wrote that the purpose of playing was 'to hold as 'twere, the mirror up to nature'. The theatre, then, as Shakespeare and his contemporaries saw it, was a drama within a drama, a small world within a larger world. This idea fitted into their whole view of man, the world and the universe. For they pictured the whole of life in terms of worlds within worlds, which influenced each other. Man was a 'microcosm' or 'little world', containing within himself all the elements of the real world, be it the natural world or society as a whole; the universe was a 'macrocosm' or 'big world' containing the same elements enlarged.

Drawing some of these threads together, we can see that religious drama had established a dramatic tradition in which moral debate and self-examination was central. The swift development of professional theatre in the sixteenth century showed the enormous enjoyment drama could provide through speech and spectacle. Shakespeare's theatre flourished as a world of entertaining fantasies, as a forum for ideas about human conduct, and as a means of moral education and spiritual growth. In *The Winter's Tale* he exploited to the full both the different types of drama familar to his audiences, with their many levels of education from illiteracy to classical scholarship, and the theatrical means at his disposal for creating truth and illusion in their minds.

2 SUMMARIES
AND
CRITICAL COMMENTARY

2.1 SUMMARY OF THE PLAY

The Winter's Tale is about two kings who were childhood friends: Leontes, King of Sicilia, who is married to Hermione and has one son, Mamillius; and Polixenes, King of Bohemia, who is also married, and has a son, Florizel. At the beginning of the play Leontes is seized with sudden jealousy. He believes that Polixenes, who is visiting him, is having an affair with Hermione, and that the baby she is about to give birth to is not his child but Polixenes's. Polixenes flees from Sicilia and returns to Bohemia, and Leontes imprisons Hermione. When the baby is born, a daughter called Perdita, he gives her to a servant to be abandoned in the desert. He puts Hermione on trial for betraying him, and denies the truth of Apollo's oracle which proclaims Hermione's innocence. His son Mamillius dies of grief, and so, apparently, does Hermione. Leontes realises his jealousy was unfounded and repents for sixteen years. Meanwhile, his daughter Perdita has been found, and is brought up as a shepherd's daughter in Bohemia. Polixenes's son Florizel meets her and they fall in love. Polixenes tries to separate the couple but they run away together to Sicilia. Polixenes pursues them there, where Perdita's true origins are discovered. A faithful servant who has been caring for Leontes takes the reconciled kings and their children to see a 'statue' of Hermione she has commissioned. The statue turns out to be the real Hermione, who is happily restored to Leontes.

2.2 CHAPTER SUMMARIES AND COMMENTARY

Act I, scene i

Summary

Archidamus, a Bohemian lord, and Camillo, a Sicilian lord, discuss the friendship between their kings and praise the young prince, Mamillius.

Commentary

At first glance this scene seems hardly necessary to the story. It establishes the place, which is the Sicilian court, and the occasion, which is the visit of King Polixenes from Bohemia, but both these facts are clearly established at the beginning of scene ii. Was Shakespeare intending just to give time for his audience to settle down before starting the main action? Perhaps, but as the play proceeds we can see, in retrospect, the importance of this opening conversation.

The scene presents a friendly relationship between Archidamus and Camillo. Archidamus feels that he and his compatriots have received such lavish hospitality that it will be difficult to match it; Camillo responds that the hospitality was given willingly and goes on to describe the warm friendship between the kings. Archidamus's praise of Mamillius, the Sicilian prince, is another compliment to Camillo. The scene establishes an atmosphere of cordiality, harmony and flowing hospitality that is a prelude to what follows.

Another feature of the scene is that we are introduced to two of the main characters, Leontes and Polixenes, indirectly. We recognise how important are the affairs of kings to their subjects, and our curiosity is aroused about these royal personages.

The conversation introduces the subject of childhood and maturity. Camillo reminds Archidamus that the two kings were 'trained together in childhood' (23-4) and only their adult responsibilities have kept them separate. They talk of the 'promise' (37) and 'hopes' (39) that Mamillius represents to the old.

Why, then, does the first scene not succeed in establishing a mood of serenity and contentment? It is because, on a level that is hard to appreciate at first, it is a scene of foreboding, written in language that disturbs. Archidamus speaks quite haltingly of his countrymen's inability to return adequate hospitality, even using the word 'shame' (8). Camillo retorts that he sets too high a price on what was given 'freely' (18). Although the exchange is a good-humoured joke, it indicates that the giving and returning of hospitality are competitive activities. Much of the scene could, in fact, be performed with a sharp sense of rivalry. And the conversation about Mamillius has a sudden reversal when Archidamus twists Camillo's meaning to point out the anxiety that arises when a king has no heir (47). Indeed, the language often twists and turns in this scene, sometimes making it difficult for the audience to follow. Archidamus speaks of the 'difference' between Bohemia and Sicilia (4). He means the dissimilarity between the two countries, but the words could also portend a difference of opinion, that is, a quarrel between (the kings of) Bohemia and Sicilia. When Camillo speaks of the affection between the two kings 'which cannot choose but branch' (25), he means the affection must grow, but the words could also portend an affection which *divides* them.

Thus the scene can be understood both as a serene prelude, contrasting with the disharmony that is to follow, *and* as a foreshadowing of that disharmony.

Act I, scene ii

Summary

This long scene is best broken into two sections for discussion.

(a) 1–185

Polixenes intends to return home to Bohemia after his nine-month stay. Leontes fails to persuade him to remain longer, Hermione succeeds. Leontes expresses his suspicion that their relationship is too close. He talks to Mamillius while watching Hermione with Polixenes, but when they notice he is upset he covers up his suspicion and lets them walk away together.

(b) 185–465

Leontes's jealousy grows. He tells his lord Camillo of Hermione's and Polixenes's adultery. Camillo does not believe him, but eventually pretends to, and agrees to poison Polixenes, on condition that Leontes takes Hermione back as his queen. Camillo tells Polixenes of the plot to murder him for adultery. He offers to help Polixenes to escape, and to be his servant.

Commentary

(a) 1–185

In less than two hundred lines Shakespeare establishes the beginning of Leontes's jealousy, from which all the subsequent events of the play spring. Clearly, this passion is sudden in its effect, but the suddenness does not necessarily make it unbelievable. We shall want to look for clues, though, from the beginning.

The audience sees the two kings for the first time, with Hermione. At least one lord, Camillo, is present, and probably several more courtiers witness the scene. Polixenes's first lines tell us he has been in Sicilia for nine months, just long enough to make Leontes's suspicion biologically plausible. During the first exchange between Polixenes and Leontes their close relationship is established. They call each other 'brother', Polixenes expresses warm thanks for Leontes's hospitality, says that Leontes would be the only person who could persuade him to stay, but insists that his affairs at home make his departure necessary. But when Hermione tries her powers of persuasion, at Leontes's request, she suggests that Leontes has spoken 'too coldly' (36) and will not accept Polixenes's reasons for leaving. She quickly teases Polixenes out of his vow and he agrees to stay (56).

In the ensuing conversation between Hermione and Polixenes, he reminisces nostalgically about his boyhood with Leontes (60-86) but Leontes himself stands apart and only re-enters the conversation at line 87, to learn that Polixenes has agreed to stay. Leontes then compares the success of Hermione's words with another occasion when she 'spoke well', and that was when she accepted his hand in marriage. She acknowledges these two occasions, and takes Polixenes's hand. It is at this moment that Leontes first expresses his judgement of the situation, 'Too hot, too hot!' (108), the exact opposite of Hermione's evaluation of *his* behaviour.

Is it true that Leontes has been too cold to his friend? How strong was Polixenes's intention to leave? Why does Hermione succeed where Leontes failed? The lines themselves do not provide clear answers to these questions. In performance actors will decide just how 'warmly' or 'coldly' to play them and the audience will evaluate according to their own sensibilities. But from this moment on there is a split in viewpoint. Leontes sees the relationship between Polixenes and Hermione differently from the way *they* perceive it, the way Camillo perceives it, and the way the audience must perceive it. His next speeches, half to himself or the audience, half to his son Mamillius, reveal his disturbed, distorted thoughts in obscure, twisted sentences (109-146).

The next step in the action is when Hermione and Polixenes notice Leontes is upset. He covers up his feelings, focuses attention on Mamillius, then deliberately lets them go off together so that he can observe their behaviour.

The most important underlying theme in this first part of the scene is the innocence of childhood. Although Hermione's advanced state of pregnancy is not mentioned until the following scene, it can be made clear to the audience visually from her first entrance. Polixenes remembers that when he and Leontes were young, they thought they would be 'boy eternal' (66) and did not look ahead to when, as men, they would lose their innocence. Mamillius, the young prince, personifies that boyhood. Leontes says his nose is 'a copy out of mine' (122), and tells Polixenes that looking at Mamillius's face makes him 'recoil twenty-three years' (154-5). Polixenes refers to the comfort he gets from his own son (165-71).

I have already noted Shakespeare's use of the terms 'cold' and 'hot' to describe behaviour in this scene. This language alerts us to the idea of winter and summer in the play. Leontes's niggardly speeches to Polixenes are somewhat wintry: Hermione's language and behaviour are warm and generous and could be said to bear fruit in that Polixenes agrees to stay. She is about to bear fruit in another sense too. Leontes speaks of bitter fruit, crab apples, when he says that 'three crabbed months had soured themselves to death' (102) before Hermione agreed to marry him. Polixenes talks of his son making 'a July's day short as December'. (169).

Another use of language that opens up a new idea in the play is when Hermione playfully threatens to keep Polixenes as a 'prisoner' instead of a 'guest' (52-7), foreshadowing Leontes's treatment of her. Looking even further ahead in the play, Polixenes twice uses language that anticipates the pastoral scenes of Act IV, when he speaks of 'the shepherd's note' (2) and compares Leontes and himself as boys to lambs in the sunshine (67-8).

(b) 185-465

Leontes expresses his revulsion at being cuckolded by his best friend. He magnifies in his imagination the huge numbers of cuckolds there may be. His language is coarse, strong and uncontrolled. He cannot pay attention to Mamillius, who had previously been his comfort. When Camillo enters he at once sets about confirming his suspicions, seeking Camillo's corroboration. When he cannot get Camillo to agree to his interpretation he turns on Camillo himself, but the courtier stands firm in his opinion of Hermione's innocence (278-83). Leontes fantasises about Polixenes and Hermione; it is becoming clear that *his* view of their relationship has become his only measure of reality; without it there is 'nothing'. He reiterates the word nine times (284-95). From now until Act III, scene ii he operates under a delusion which Camillo here calls 'this diseased opinion' (296). Everything he does is logical but wrong-headed. Thus, if Camillo contradicts Leontes's opinion, *he* must be a liar (298-9). The speed with which Leontes's jealousy has grown is shown when Camillo still doesn't know who is the man implicated in Hermione's so-called infidelity (304). Camillo makes one last avowal of his belief in Hermione's innocence (320-2), but Leontes brushes him aside in a speech of sharp irony (325-32) in which he suggests that no man would be so 'muddy' or 'unsettled' as to invent something so painful to himself. Yet this is precisely what he *has* done. Truth and untruth have turned topsy-turvy in his mind. In actuality it is only now that Camillo does lie, pretending to believe Leontes and agreeing to poison Polixenes merely in order to gain some breathing space.

Immediately Leontes has left, Camillo reveals his real intention. He convinces Polixenes of Leontes's sudden change of heart, reinforcing in the audience's mind the firm hold that Leontes's delusion has taken. When Polixenes asks how Leontes's jealousy grew, Camillo's reply is pure common sense, and it also helps the audience move forward to the consequences and not back to the cause of the trouble:

> I know not: but I am sure 'tis safer to
> Avoid what's grown than question how 'tis born (431-2).

Polixenes pauses to appreciate the size and scope of the calamity (450-6) then hastens away.

Shakespeare's treatment of time in this long scene has been skilful. Leontes's jealousy is built up in stages, so that the audience has the illusion of it growing for a period. Yet the forward thrust of the action has been as relentless as his passion, leading to the precarious situation where Hermione will have to face Leontes's madness without the protection of either Polixenes or Camillo.

The language in the second half of the scene is full of images of disease, infection and impurity that contrast sharply with the 'innocence' depicted earlier. The idea of 'growth' has been applied to the spread of evil and corruption, where before it was used to suggest breeding and fruitfulness.

Another idea that has been introduced is that of 'playing'. Leontes tells Mamillius to go and play and then explores other meanings of the word (186-7). He accuses Hermione of play-acting as in a theatre, and 'so disgraced a part', that she will be hissed. We can see that it is really *he* who plays a disgraced part.

Act II, scene i

Summary
Hermione is enjoying domestic peace with Mamillius and her ladies-in-waiting. Leontes discovers the flight of Polixenes and Camillo and believes they meant to murder him and take his crown. He separates Mamillius from Hermione, then accuses her of adultery and conspiracy. Despite her denials he sends her to prison. Two of his lords try to make him see he has misjudged her. He tells them he has sent messengers to Apollo's oracle at Delphos to confirm the truth of his accusations.

Commentary
The scene begins in a mood of gentle playfulness. Mamillius teases the ladies like a little man and they enjoy it. There is talk of Hermione's pregnancy. Then he starts to tell his mother a story. She suggests it should be 'merry' but he decides 'a sad tale's best for winter' (24-5). This line has the effect of distancing the audience, and making the contentment in the scene quite poignant. We may remember the title of the play and that

Leontes is creating a winter's tale himself, full of imaginary evil, like the 'sprites and goblins' (26) Mamillius tells of. The boy's story begins 'There was a man - Dwelt by a churchyard' (29-30). In the last act of the play the audience will see Leontes living by the churchyard, repenting the deeds he is now about to commit. Mamillius's tale will have come true, like a prophecy.

Mamillius engrosses his mother with the story, while Leontes's entrance breaks the mood harshly for the audience. His reaction to the news of Camillo's escape with Polixenes is predictable: he sees it as confirmation of his opinion, developing an instant theory of conspiracy without even stating what evidence he has for it. At this point he expresses the full horror of his own situation with a vividness that may arouse some sympathy in the audience, for the nightmare he is enduring (39-45). Leontes thinks himself 'infected' as if by a poisonous spider. But for the audience he is the spider, about to poison his innocent family who don't yet see his evil. It seems that nothing can be done to shake the firm foundation on which he now builds all his suspicions as if they were certainties.

When Leontes now openly accuses Hermione of carrying Polixenes's child, she thinks at first it is 'sport' (58), but she quickly makes a clear denial. She tries to make him see that he is mistaken, that he is doing her wrong. It is easiest to evaluate her behaviour by what she does *not* do. She does not weep or grow angry; she does not plead with him, or go on lengthily insisting that she is right and he is wrong; she does not appeal for support from the courtiers, nor call for revenge on Leontes for his public insults and unjust treatment of her. Instead she summons patience (106-7), asks the lords to make up their own minds about her and requests that 'the king's will be performed'. She knows that it is better to be punished undeservedly than to have committed the crime (118-21).

After Hermione has gone, the lord Antigonus speaks forcefully to Leontes. In a sense his reaction parallels Leontes's: he says that Hermione's guilt would make all women guilty (137-9), would make him, Antigonus, wish to produce no heirs (143-9), and would destroy all faith in honesty (154-7). Leontes would agree with these exaggerated claims, but Antigonus builds them upon the important word '*if*'. The whole structure of Leontes's world now rests on this one false supposition that Hermione is guilty. At this stage of the play he has started to impose that structure on everyone else around him.

At the same time that Leontes's belief begins to affect his world, some ideas of powers *beyond* him are introduced in the scene: Hermione believes that 'some ill planet reigns' (105), and she must be patient until 'the heavens look/With an aspect more favourable' (105-6). The lord stakes his life on his belief that the queen is 'spotless/In th'eyes of heaven' (131-2). We learn, too, that Apollo's oracle is to be consulted, though Leontes says that this is just to convince those who do not yet accept the truth of what he *knows* (189-93).

Act II, scene ii

Summary

Paulina, a lady of the court, visits the prison where Hermione is lodged. The gaoler will not let her in, but summons Hermione's attendant, Emilia, who tells Paulina that the Queen has given birth to a daughter. Paulina suggests that she should take the baby girl to Leontes in hopes of softening his heart. Emilia agrees, saying that Hermione had thought of this plan already. Paulina persuades the gaoler it is lawful to pass the baby over.

Commentary

The first eight lines of this short scene are very simple, contrasting sharply with the twisted language of Leontes, and the sense of frustration this raised in other characters and in the audience. A new character, Paulina, is introduced, though for some lines her identity remains uncertain. She summons the gaoler in words that express confidence that her position will carry command. Then she comments on Hermione's situation (2-4), in words that remind us that the true 'gaoler' is Leontes himself, the true prison is his court. The gaoler confirms the impression that Paulina is a woman of some position and reputation (5-6). For a moment it seems as if this strong woman's common sense and directness may prevail. The gaoler's plain refusal is like a door slamming. Paulina's language alters, becoming less sure, but she pursues her intention to make contact with Hermione, though it will have to be indirect. Hermione's attendant Emilia is summoned, and so, as with several important incidents in this story, the audience does not *see* Hermione but learns of her condition through hearsay, and of the birth of her baby daughter.

Although the gaoler is still silently present, the action carried forward in the scene is now entirely concerned with women. Emilia is the go-between who links the passive, suffering Hermione with the active, aggressive Paulina. Paulina decides Leontes's madness must be dealt with by a woman: she will speak to him, expressing a woman's anger (29-34). Then she thinks of another way of changing his mind: she will use the baby as a go-between, letting the sight of the innocent child soften his harshness. The closeness between Paulina and Hermione is indicated by the fact that Hermione had already thought of this plan (50-1). It remains only to persuade the gaoler to let them take the child, and here Paulina uses her wits well, arguing that the baby herself, unborn at the time of Hermione's imprisonment, is not subject to Leontes's sentence. So, by the end of the scene, there is hope that Paulina's eloquence and intelligence, combined with the sight of the innocent baby, will change Leontes's view and treatment of Hermione.

In this scene several ideas that have been introduced before are developed. The birth of Hermione's baby brings another innocent child into the story, but there is a double meaning in the word 'innocent' (24). When applied to a baby it means not only a lack of guilt but a lack of knowledge of any sin – a child is not even conscious of right and wrong. Whereas, when applied to Hermione, 'innocent' means she is not guilty of the specific crimes Leontes accuses her of. Paulina uses the word 'advocate' (39) which anticipates the court of law we shall see later in the play, and the need to have Hermione's case pleaded. The importance of go-betweens in the scene links with this: Paulina will be an advocate for Hermione, but she sees that the baby may be a more effective one, though, paradoxically, unable to speak.

Other words that have a double meaning in the scene are Emilia's 'a thriving issue' (45). She uses them to mean Paulina's plan, which she hopes will lead to the *happy result* of changing Leontes's mind. But 'issue' also means a child or descendant, so the words apply also to the *healthy baby* Hermione has brought forth.

Near the end of the scene, when Paulina persuades the gaoler to let her take the baby, she introduces another important idea. She reminds us of another power *beyond* Leontes's, and that is the power of Nature (59-61). The child is not Leontes's prisoner. Rather, she was Nature's prisoner while in the womb. Now, through birth, she has been set 'free' by the laws of Nature. Paulina persuades the gaoler that 'the law and process of great Nature' is above any law of Leontes's.

Act II, scene iii

Summary

Leontes, unable to sleep, ponders how to remove the cause of his restlessness. Paulina enters with the baby, breaking through the lords, including her husband Antigonus, who have been told to admit no one. She faces Leontes's anger, lays the baby before him, and shows the lords how like Leontes it is. He tries to have her thrown out, but she leaves of her own free will, leaving the baby. Leontes tells Antigonus to have the child burnt, then relents and makes him take it to a desert place and abandon it. Antigonus leaves with the baby. News comes that the messengers sent to the oracle have landed back in the kingdom. Leontes orders a public session where Hermione will be formally accused and tried.

Commentary

From the world of women and prison, the scene moves back to Leontes, who has constructed a prison inside his own head. His belief in Hermione's guilt has brought him nothing but pain and turmoil, but he will not let anything or anyone in to cure the pain. His courtiers stand around, cowed and helpless, no longer even trying to change his mind. When Paulina enters, the audience sees a reversal of conventional sex roles where men are strong and dominant, while women are gentle and submissive. Paulina scolds the lords for creeping about like shadows, encouraging Leontes's delusion (33-6). Her arrival and bold manner drive him to the very peak of his passion. He has given special instructions that she was not to come to him, apparently anticipating this visit (43-4). His fury takes the form of taunting Antigonus for not being able to rule his wife. He tries to get Paulina removed by physical force. But either because of their natural courtesy, or because of her masculine combative behaviour, they will not do it. Baulked for the first time, Leontes unleashes a stream of insults at her: 'a mankind witch' (67), 'a most intelligencing bawd' (68), 'crone' (76) 'a callot of boundless tongue' (90-1), 'a gross hag' (108); and at Antigonus for letting 'Dame Partlet' (75) rule him: 'dotard' and 'woman-tired' (74), 'lozel' (108).

Paulina insists on carrying out her errand. She shows him the baby sent by his 'good queen' (58-9) and confirms that it is really Leontes's child by pointing out its likeness to him. Leontes's diction remains crude as he calls the baby a bastard, a 'brat' (92) and its mother a 'dam' (94). Paulina's language remains dignified even in her firmness (76-9). In the crucial passage where she describes the baby's features (97-107), there are two dramatic elements to note. First, that she uses the masculine pronoun throughout, to emphasise that each of the baby girl's features is 'his', thus driving home the similarity between father and daughter. The other point is that we do not know from the text what Leontes is doing at this moment, as she speaks on without interruption. Is he standing speechless with rage? Or is he listening spellbound like the lords, as Paulina looks from child to man and from man to child? He does break in at last, telling Antigonus he should be hanged for not being able to stop her speaking. Antigonus's reply is the only moment of humour in the scene, as he tells Leontes ruefully that if every husband was hanged for that, the king would have very few subjects (108-11)! Like Leontes's earlier reference to Paulina as 'Dame Partlet' Antigonus's remark conjures up the traditional role reversal where the husband is henpecked. The real situation of a king disowning his royal wife and daughter is strikingly different from the vulgar insults to which Leontes has sunk. His behaviour is, as Paulina says, that of a 'most unworthy and unnatural lord' (112). She reminds him of his position as monarch, coming near to accusing him of tyranny (115-9) that will slur his reputation in the world. After this, though his rage does not abate, his language is less gross.

Paulina exits of her own free will, leaving Leontes with the problem of what to do with the child. He wavers over his decision, seemingly unsure how his rage at Paulina and Antigonus should affect his treatment of Hermione's 'bastard'. When that is settled, and the dreadful oath sworn by Antigonus, the scene ends quickly with the announcement of the messengers' return from Delphos, which prompts Leontes to order a public trial. He says it will be 'just and open' (204), but his very next words contradict that by anticipating its verdict.

Much of Leontes's behaviour in the scene has been the uttering of pure rage. He has threatened Paulina, Antigonus and the baby with fire, but the one punishment he keeps returning to is that of Hermione, the cause of all his anguish, whose removal will put his mind at rest. It is as if he is ill and her death will cure the illness. The punishment he keeps threatening is *fire*, as if he hopes to burn out the evil. But Paulina offers another kind of cure. She uses the language of medicine (36-9), as Camillo did in I.ii.296-7. She calls herself his 'physician' (54) and her final words to the lords are that their way of handling the king 'will never do him good' (127-8). In II.i Paulina's actions seemed motivated by her love for the queen, but in this scene her desire is to cure the king. He refuses her treatment; it does not seem that she has done as much good as the loyalty of his lords, which ultimately soothes the worst of the wrath she enflamed. The idea of illness is carried through Mamillius, too, who has fallen sick.

Act III, scene i

Summary
Cleomenes and Dion, the king's messengers, returning from Delphos with Apollo's words sealed up unread, pause in their journey back to the court and share their impressions of the oracle.

Commentary
This short scene carries the story no further – the audience already knows the messengers are on their way back – yet its contribution to the play is considerable. It provides the audience with an impression of the oracle and gives some respite from the relentless sweep of Leontes's anger. For a more detailed examination of the meaning and effect of the scene, see the specimen passage in Chapter 6.

Act III, scene ii

Summary
Hermione, on trial before Leontes, proclaims her innocence, which he rejects. She calls on Apollo to judge her. The oracle is brought in and read. It clears her of any blemish, together with Polixenes, Camillo and the baby; pronounces Leontes a jealous tyrant; and ends with a prophecy that the king will die without an heir, if that which is lost be not found. Leontes rejects the oracle, but at that moment news is brought that Mamillius is dead, fulfilling the first part of the prophecy. Leontes acknowledges

Apollo's anger and admits his injustice. Hermione collapses and is carried off with her attendants. Leontes begs Apollo's pardon and promises to reconcile himself with Polixenes, Hermione and Camillo. But Paulina enters to tell him that the queen is dead. He vows to repent daily at the graveside of his queen and son as long as he has life and strength to do so.

Commentary

The previous scene briefly delayed this climactic scene in the drama that Leontes has set in motion himself. Suspense and curiosity have thus been aroused.

A trial is a public event, conducted in this case in the open air; marital relations are private. Shakespeare exploits to the full the tension between public and private in the scene. Leontes begins by playing out his public role with some solemnity. His language is chillingly formal, continually using the royal 'we', even describing Hermione as 'our wife'.

At the impersonal command to 'produce the prisoner', Hermione is brought on. Without any royal comforts she is simply a woman just risen from childbirth, thrown into the coldness of the open air court (104). That her entrance produces a sympathetic reaction from the courtiers is clear from the officer's command for silence. The indictment is read. The formality of the proceedings prevents her from making any direct appeal to her husband at first. She is well aware of the futility of her situation, where the plea 'not guilty' rests on her integrity, which is being called in question (22-8). But whereas in II.i she had to accept defeat when she recognised the strength of Leontes's false perception, now she is more conscious of her own strengths and takes him on at his own game.

Her first speech is phrased in legal terms and presents her plight as sympathetically and persuasively as any advocate for her defence would do. It requires all her skill in eloquence, her courage and her dignity to deliver. It falls on deaf ears, however, for Leontes responds with typically contorted logic. He bandies words with her in a way that indicates this is not the just and open trial he promised in II.ii, for he is taking the triple role of judge, prosecutor and plaintiff. There is no disinterested party to whom she can address herself. She shifts therefore to a more personal approach, directly addressing Leontes as her husband. Her poignant account of the situation reminds the audience of the triple bonds that Leontes has torn, between himself and Hermione, between Hermione and Polixenes and between Polixenes and himself.

When Leontes insists that she was involved in a plot, presumably to murder him, Hermione sees that there is no communication between them (80-1). She gives up any hope of convincing him and prepares to relinquish her life. Not recognising her new sense of the situation, Leontes continues to react from within his limited perception, reiterating the bastardy, telling her the brat has been cast out (it is not clear if she already knew this), and threatening her with death. But by reducing her to despair Leontes has lost his power to cause her fear and pain. Now she rather welcomes death than fears it. We have seen how Leontes gave himself a false sense of identity and reality (I.ii). Here we see how Hermione sets no value on her life because Leontes has snatched away everything that made it worthwhile. She lists those things starting with his favour, which she calls the 'crown and comfort of my life'. Leontes, too, suffers the worst pain through losing her. The description of her unhappy position shows Hermione at her most private, personal and vulnerable. It seems as if she is giving up. Then at the line 'Therefore proceed' (108), she changes tack again, coming back to the question of her honour, which is public.

Speaking now with all the dignity of her rank, Hermione takes the situation back from a personal argument to a formal trial, turning the tables on Leontes by accusing *him*.

If she is condemned through nothing more than his 'surmises' (112) it will be 'rigour and not law' (114). She makes a double plea for justice, appealing to the whole court, and through them to the higher authority of Apollo (114–16). Does she know the oracle has been consulted? Possibly. But she may be assuming that her appeal will mean a delay. Either way, it is a moment of excitement and tension. Leontes has been pushing the proceedings so forcefully that the court and the audience must feel apprehension that he isn't going to have the oracle's pronouncement brought in at all, but now his bluff is called. He must let it be read to avoid the accusation of tyranny.

The next twenty-five lines pack in so many changes that the dramatic tension is raised to a level of higher excitement than at any other point except the final scene. There is the suspense of waiting for Cleomenes and Dion, then the delay while they take the oath, then at last the breaking of the seals and the reading of the oracle in all its devastating simplicity. Leontes's blasphemous rejection is immediately followed by the news of Mamillius's death. At the very word 'dead' Leontes suddenly changes. He interprets the death of his son as Apollo's revenge for his blasphemy, and punishment for his injustice. Hermione faints. Immediately he demonstrates his recovery from jealousy, ordering that she be taken care of, with softer words than he has used throughout the play so far – 'Beseech you, tenderly...' (152). As he begs pardon of Apollo, promises restitution and recounts the wrongs he has done, the great change in him alerts us to the fact that the whole first movement of the play is over, although the scene proceeds further.

Looking at the trial in the first part of the scene, it is important to note its theatricality. We noted Leontes's use of theatrical terms in I.ii. He himself has invented a drama of Hermione's adultery: the trial is a presentation of that drama, for which he has already planned the end, her death. Hermione points out that her unhappiness is greater than anything devised for the theatre (35-7). Her lines make us aware that she has been forced to play in Leontes's drama. A play, in being separate from the reality of everyday life, is not unlike a dream. Hermione says Leontes treats her life like a dream (81). We are again made aware that he has created a reality that is like a drama inside in his own head. Hermione's speeches are often the-atrical in another sense. We have seen how clearly she depicts her own predicament. She sees her situation as a spectator would. She even envisages her father seeing her plight. This objective eye, the ability to see herself in perspective, is in marked contrast to Leontes, who is far too immersed in his own drama to be self-aware. Her ability to see herself comes from her faith that she *is* in a kind of drama. For there are spectators, 'powers divine' who 'behold our human actions' (28-9). This faith gives her the confidence and courage to express her innocence. The events of the scene show us that these powers, represented here by Apollo, do more than behold. They may actually intervene and guide the drama of human action. It is this that Leontes has forgotten, intent on bringing the drama *he* has devised, to its conclusion. It takes the death of Mamillius to make him recognise that he has been living in a fantasy.

This scene introduces the idea of sleep, waking and death, that are to be important in other parts of the play. We have already noted Hermione's use of the word 'dreams', which Leontes takes up. She speaks also of 'all proofs *sleeping* else/but what your jealousies *awake*' (112-3). Mamillius's death has the effect of 'waking' Leontes from his dream, but immediately Hermione falls in a faint, which Paulina sees as death (149), though Leontes believes she will recover. He does not know in what sense these words are both true and false. He will have to experience her death before she can recover. When he asks that Hermione receive 'some rem-edies for life' (153), his words recall the idea of sickness and medicine already introduced.

After Hermione is taken off, Leontes begs for Apollo's pardon, probably on his knees. His reversal has been as abrupt and swift as the beginning of his jealousy. Is it for that reason unbelievable? Sudden conversion or change of heart is rare and improbable, but it happens. A powerful actor can make this rare and improbable event convincing to an audience, so that they will wonder at it, but believe it.

In his first speech after his return to sanity Leontes gives most of his attention, not to his chief victims, Hermione or Polixenes, but to his servant Camillo, drawing a sharp contrast between Camillo's piety and his black deeds (171-2). Preceding as it does the re-entrance of Paulina, the speech makes a link between these two characters whose function in the play is to turn evil to good. Leontes's new view of Camillo shows that his perceptions have cleared. He is at last cured of his 'diseased opinion'. But the consequences of his jealousy are still reverberating in the world and cannot be cured so quickly.

Paulina now re-enters with news that radically changes the new direction of the drama. Leontes was moving towards the idea of reconciliation with the three he has wronged. Now she breaks in to confront him with the full picture of the wrongs done through his tyranny and jealousy (179-80). Far from seeking to 'cure' him as she has in II.iii, now she wishes him to think about what he has done 'and then run mad indeed, stark mad!' (183). She forces her wish upon him, recounting his wrongs one by one to a now receptive Leontes. Starting with the betrayal of Polixenes and the dishonouring of Camillo, she adds the wrongs he has not yet named: the abandonment of his daughter and the death of Mamillius, working up to the climactic announcement of the queen's death.

Shakespeare gives the audience no hint that her news might be false. This allows the final scene, when Hermione comes to life again, to retain its essential mystery.

To Paulina, Leontes is still a tyrant. She advises him not even to repent, but only to despair (207-10). These lines are the more startling when you consider that Shakespeare's audience was a Christian society whose chief tenet of faith was that the worst sinner can be redeemed through repentance. She insists, with exaggerated expressiveness, that no repentance could save him (210-14). The first indication she gets of the change in Leontes is when, instead of begging her to stop, he asks her to go on with her bitter words. At this reversal of his earlier attitude, she too changes, saying she is sorry for her outspoken insistence on what's past (218-26). Addressing him courteously for the first time in the play, she asks his forgiveness, promising to say no more, yet simultaneously breaking that promise (226-32) as she *does* remind him again of his wife and children, and adds her husband too. But Leontes now prefers her truth to being pitied. In his last speech he moves the action to a kind of resolution very different from the headlong rush of disastrous events he precipitated until now. He plans a regime of shame and sorrow, centred on the graves of his wife and son: a narrow existence that will be limited in a different way from the narrowness of outlook imposed by his jealousy.

Just as Hermione's speeches dominated the first part of the scene, Paulina's dominate the second part. Much of her language brings up ideas and associations that relate to other parts of the play. Her reference to the fire and burning that Leontes, as tyrant, might inflict upon her (174-5) remind us of other heat images used about his jealousy. Her allusion to boys and girls (181) keeps the idea of childhood present at the back of our minds. She continues the idea of poison (188). She depicts the plight of the baby, 'casting forth to crows' (191) more graphically than it can be represented on the stage in the following scene, and links that with the word 'monstrous' (190), thus anticipating the bear. Her mention of her husband (230) will also link with the next scene. She considers Leontes worse than a devil (192) which perhaps accounts for her conviction that nothing can bring him back in favour with the gods. In her picture of Leontes's penance (210-4) the reference to 'barren mountain' anticipates the bleak setting of the following scene, and also contrasts with the images and incidents of pregnancy and fruitfulness in other parts of the play. She continues with 'still winter/In storm perpetual', also words which anticipate the next scene, and at the same time indicate that we are at the most wintry part of the play, in the midst of death and despair.

Act III, scene iii

Summary

Antigonus's ship lands on the desert shore of Bohemia. He tells how Hermione came to him in a vision, telling him to bring the child here and call it 'Perdita' (the girl who is lost); and warning him that he will never see his wife again. He lays the baby down with a bundle of clothes, a box of gold and jewels and a written account of her. A storm begins. He is chased away by a bear. An old shepherd comes on, looking for his sheep. He finds the baby. His son arrives, telling how the storm has wrecked a ship and Antigonus has been eaten by the bear. They take up the baby and her belongings and prepare to set off for home.

Commentary

The scene shows several important changes and at the same time is firmly linked with what has gone before. Antigonus's entrance with the baby tells the audience at once that the story has shifted to follow *her* fortunes. The action is to be concerned with the 'issue' in that double sense of the word, meaning (1) *what happens next* (to) (2) *the offspring* (of) Hermione and Leontes. The location, too, switches to the desert shore, a landscape not unlike the barren mountain mentioned by Paulina, as noted in the previous scene. In Shakespeare's theatre this change of scene was made almost entirely through words and through the audience's imaginations, not through scenery. We need to remember that although the geography has changed in this scene, the previous scene with Leontes was like a desert too, a desert of the mind. The very first words tell the audience that *this* desert does not offer the baby quite so hopeless a fate as Leontes wished upon her, for it is in Bohemia. Just as Camillo saved Polixenes from the death Leontes prescribed for him, the baby may be saved by Antigonus's choice of a desert place. Nevertheless, the mariner's words, announcing the imminent storm, convey the grimness of the occasion. Both he and Antigonus interpret the storm as an expression of divine anger. (Both are ignorant of the death of Mamillius, which Leontes interpreted as divine anger too.)

Antigonus dismisses the mariner so that he can accomplish his dreadful mission alone, then recounts his vision. The picture conjured up by the words is as important as the picture before the audience's eyes. They share Antigonus's vision of Hermione, coming to him as he slept in his ship's cabin. It is left doubtful if the vision was the 'real' ghost of Hermione or a dream. The sense of unreality in the whole description anticipates her later transformation into a statue. It also evokes the description by Dion of the oracle at Delphos, especially her white robes 'like very sanctity' (23). Hermione's speech in his vision is like a divine message itself, giving instructions and a prophecy, though her weeping and shrieks express more human suffering. Antigonus inclines towards believing his vision, accepting it as the real spirit of Hermione, who must therefore be dead. His interpretation helps to confirm the audience's belief in Hermione's death, though he links it with what the audience knows to be false, the belief that the baby is the child of Polixenes.

As he lays the child down, signs of hope and despair alternate: the gold, the clothes and the letter offer the possibility she may survive and be preserved, but the storm begins, emphasising the slimness of her chances. Antigonus thinks himself accursed for having to carry out his oath. He may have inadvertently cursed himself in another way, for in recognising 'thy mother's fault' (50), he becomes the only character besides Leontes to have believed in Hermione's guilt.

The stage direction 'Exit pursued by bear' (58) is probably the most famous in Shakespeare, with its combination of horror and farce. That very combination is an appropriate expression of this moment in the play, where tragedy and comedy meet, where tears begin to turn to laughter. In production this moment can be terrifying or comical. Shakespeare's audience would have seen bears as both dangerous, frightening beasts and as something to be made sport of.

There are other possible significances for the bear. It represents a horrifying danger, and could be said to symbolise Leontes or to be an extension of his evil in monstrous form. But since the bear is a hibernating animal, which spends the winter in a cave, its emergence may be thought to symbolise spring, and the return of life. Shakespeare does not bring out either of these meanings in the language and may never have intended them, but the possibilities are present in the incident itself.

The old shepherd now enters, with his grumblings about youth. His speech places wrong deeds in a much less direful context than the play has previously shown. At this moment youth's only crime is, as he mistakenly supposes, to have scared away his sheep. He will find them again, just as he finds the child, lost through another kind of mistake. The audience's suspense is short-lived but strong, waiting for him to discover the baby abandoned by another old man only moments before. When he finds it, his response is very like that of Antigonus: he assumes it is a bastard, but feels pity for it. His kind nature is established by the fact that he decides to take it up before he discovers the gold.

The shepherd's son, who now enters, is called simply 'Clown', his name indicating his main function as a comic character; he recounts the shipwreck and the death of Antigonus. Another example of information conveyed to the audience and other characters through story-telling rather than dramatic presentation. The attention is less on the dreadful deaths of the mariners and Antigonus than on the story-teller himself. His manner of telling the stories is so absurd that he inadvertently turns his narration to comedy for the audience. He switches from the shipwreck to the bear and back again, searching wildly for appropriate language from his own limited experience, coming up with homely images of a bodkin, a beer barrel foaming over, and a flapdragon; and courteously alludes to poor Antigonus the nobleman as a 'gentleman'.

The old shepherd reacts to their plight with sympathy (104, 109–10), then shows the baby to the clown with the memorable comment: 'Now bless thyself: thou met'st with things dying, I with things new-born' (115–16). Unknowingly, he has summed up the action of the play until now, and pushed it forward.

When they find the gold, the old shepherd assumes it is fairy gold. His interpretation brings out the idea of belief and superstition in the play. The audience knows it was human action at work, not the supernatural. The scene ends on a note of optimism. It has been a 'lucky' day, and they are both off to perform the 'good deeds' (140–1) of getting the baby home and Antigonus buried.

Thus the scene moves from storms, death and despair to hope and light-heartedness; from tragedy to comedy. The transitional nature of the scene is emphasised in several ways. There is the change from evil and death (the casting out of Perdita, the apparent death of Hermione, the deaths of mariners and Antigonus) to good (the discovery of Perdita by a good and kind old man); a change from the high life of the court to the low life of the countryside; a change from tragedy to comedy. The old shepherd's words: 'thou met'st with things dying, I with things new-born' is a key line in the play as a whole. Youth and age are balanced against each other, for it was the old man who found the baby, while the young boy witnessed death. This setting-up of opposites is typical of the scene. Shakespeare keeps asking us to look at things first one way, then another. Hope and despair alternate at many points. The bear may appear monstrous or ridiculous during its brief appearance. Significantly, the old shepherd starts his speech by carping about adolescence, the age when we are half child, half adult. Notice too, how his and the clown's eyes and bodies must swivel from side to side following the muddled story of the sea and land. The clown's story contains, indeed, the fullest expression of these violent turnabouts. The tossing and turning of the ship itself represents this movement. Hermione has been described by Antigonus as a 'vessel' (21) with eyes like 'two spouts'. The confusion of sky, sea and land shows us that while we have at last left behind the destructive element of fire, the other three elements are all mingled together: air (associated with spirits), water (associated with weeping) and earth. The speech itself evokes horror and laughter alternately.

Act IV, scene i

Summary

'Time' personified as an old man with wings and an hour-glass, tells the audience he is passing over a gap of sixteen years. He sets the scene in Bohemia, reminds the audience of the existence of the King's son, Florizel, then tells them that the story will focus on Perdita. He wishes the audience a good time, and departs.

Commentary

It was not unusual in the drama of Shakespeare's time to have a narrator, or chorus, who spoke directly to the audience to introduce scene and action. Shakespeare himself used the device several times. Usually, though, such a character appears at the beginning of a play. Making his one appearance halfway through the play, Time has a surprising effect here, even though the figure of Time as an old man would have been familar to Shakespeare's audience. Time breaks the close involvement which the audience may have felt in Leontes's story in three ways: (1) as narrator, he comes between them and the events of the story; (2) the story itself becomes discontinuous as Time abruptly jumps sixteen years; (3) Leontes is dismissed in two lines, all attention being directed on the events surrounding his daughter in Bohemia. Yet the audience has also been prepared for Time's appearance in various ways. He is the third old man to address the audience directly. He completes a transition that was begun by Antigonus's scene. The Bohemian setting, the focus on Perdita, the turning towards happier events, all these have been established already. The mention of Florizel gives the audience a hint of what the next event might be, since he is so obviously suited by circumstances to fall in love with Perdita. Yet in spite of preparing the audience to shift their attention from Leontes, the first part of the next scene will be very much connected with him.

Time tells us very little, then, that the surrounding scenes do not convey. The only action in the scene is the turning of the hour-glass, so that the audience can share the experience of watching the 'sands of time' running through. Much of his speech is an explanation of the whole idea of Time.

First of all, Time reminds us that everyone is affected by the passing of time and what it brings. It is not clearly good or bad, for it both 'makes and unfolds error' (2)' He has the power to 'o'erthrow law . . . and custom' (4-9). This explanation parallels Leontes's action, for his error did consist in taking too much power and in overthrowing law and custom. Time presents himself as a force present throughout history. This is a way of reminding us that all time in the past was once the present. He emphasises the present by assuring the audience that he is the power that brings in 'the freshest things now reigning' (13). These words, spoken by such an ancient-looking figure, take us back to the previous scene, where we saw one old man bring in a baby, and another old man take her off. He goes on to complete the thought by saying the passing of time also makes the vividness of the present become 'stale' as we look back on it (12-13). This prepares us to look at the freshness of some of the following scenes with an awareness that that quality is temporary, specifically the youthful innocence of Florizel and Perdita. In turning to these two characters he claims he has already mentioned Polixenes's son (21-2). This is either an error on Shakespeare's part, or it means that Time should be seen as the presenter of the whole play, responsible for what was said about Florizel in Act I.

The style of the scene is in marked contrast to the rest of the play. For Shakespeare's audience it would have sounded old-fashioned. The presentation of abstract characters like Time was typical of an earlier tradition of drama. Rhyming couplets make the speech progress rather haltingly and the pedantic tone makes Time's character like a dull old teacher or preacher. Yet he seems to be aware of that, acknowledging (14-15) that his tale is stale. The archaic quality of the scene underlines its theme: Shakespeare is demonstrating that in drama too, old ways give place to new, but the old has a contribution to make.

Act IV, scene ii

Summary

Polixenes refuses Camillo's request to return to Leontes, and turns both their attentions to his son. He has discovered Florizel's frequent visits to an old shepherd and his beautiful daughter. Suspecting an unsuitable romance, he decides to disguise himself in order to investigate. Camillo agrees to go with him.

Commentary

The scene is, as Time has already told us, in 'fair Bohemia', its fairness being expressed not through its beauty but through its reasonableness, compared with the *un*reasonable Sicilian court. The audience is reintroduced to two characters, now sixteen years older, who disappeared precipitately at the end of Act I. Very little happens, but two decisions are made. Polixenes's decision to discover who Florizel has been seeing is set within the choice Camillo has to make between two masters. Both decisions push the story towards an eventual reconciliation between the two kings, but both characters believe they are moving *away* from anything to do with Leontes. The audience is put in a position of superior knowledge, with the possibility of predicting at least part of the outcome.

While foreknowledge gives some satisfaction, it may not at first compensate for the slow progress of the scene, which is mainly due to Polixenes's longwindedness. Yet his very tediousness needs to be understood as a welcome contrast to Leontes's frenetic activity in the first part of the play. Time has slowed down. When this king's wishes are crossed, he tries persuasion; when he harbours suspicions he tests them instead of taking them as proof. And the testing itself, involving disguise, is likely to provide entertainment.

The dramatic situation in the scene, with the king trying to persuade the loyal servant Camillo to do his will, is in some ways parallel to I.ii.211–349, when Leontes tried to get Camillo to poison Polixenes. It would be a useful exercise to compare and contrast these passages, looking at the two king/servant relationships. Throughout Act IV Camillo's choices will parallel and often guide the course of the action. Now, he turns his attention away from Sicilia until such time as he sees a possibility of past and present being combined productively.

The language of this scene echoes the somewhat dull action it presents. Since a king is present we might have expected the scene to be in blank verse (see page 55) but it is in prose. Blank verse is not spoken again until the appearance of Florizel and Perdita. Camillo and Polixenes communicate mainly through factual information and abstract discussion. The exceptions are worth noting: Polixenes's mention of 'sickness' and 'death', Camillo desiring to 'lay his bones' in Sicilia, and the word 'afresh' used in Polixenes's remembrance of Leontes. By the style of the language Shakespeare emphasises that Polixenes and Camillo are now ageing men, for whom, in Time's words, the 'glistering' of their youth has become 'stale'. For an impression of true freshness we must wait for the appearance of the youthful prince and 'princess' whose dominance over much of the ensuing act will rival that of Polixenes.

Act IV, scene iii

Summary

Autolycus introduces himself to the audience. When the clown enters, on his way to buy food for a sheep-shearing feast, Autolycus robs him, pretending to have been beaten up and robbed by 'Autolycus' himself.

Commentary

Little in the play so far has prepared the audience for the character of Autolycus, who entirely controls this scene. It is a comic interlude, refreshing the audience and at the same time adding to the effect of Florizel's and Perdita's entrance by delaying it. Since Shakespeare wrote it to amuse the audience of his own time, he used a lot of slang and topical language which makes it difficult for a modern reader or audience to get the jokes and allusions immediately. But the tricking of the clown, which forms the main part of the scene, is done through physical actions and reactions which can easily be appreciated in a good performance.

Autolycus's simple folk song sets the scene away from the sophistication of the court. In it, Shakespeare leads the audience through the seasons, just as he led them through the years with Time's speech. The first verse is about the coming of spring after the winter which we may equate with the first part of the play. The second verse develops the picture of life in the countryside. The third verse pushes on towards summer, which is the season in which the scene is set.

Autolycus gets his comic effects through his honesty and lack of shame about his tricks and thefts. He did not enter the scene with a clear intention, as most characters up to now have done. But the sight of the clown, who is just entering, immediately gives the possibility of a 'prize' (31). The clown is sixteen years older than in II.iii, so he must be at least in his twenties: his slowness of mind is comical. He is a perfect victim for Autolycus, who waits patiently for the right moment to lay his trap.

The clown's long speech about the sheep-shearing feast is probably to himself rather than to the audience; it gives a vivid impression of the preparations undertaken by 'the mistress of the feast'. Having heard of Perdita's grace, the audience now gets a much more fleshed out picture of a young girl working busily to provide hospitality for her father's sheep-shearers. The picture belongs to the world of the English countryside which Shakespeare knew well and he gives specific details that help the audience to focus on the basic commodities of such a feast: the foods and spices needed for more lavish dishes than usual, the flowers, the entertainment of songs and dances provided by the guests themselves. Warmth of the sun, warmth of hospitality, fragrant smells and flavoursome foods, harmony, companionship and unsophisticated pleasures - these are the prospects conjured up by the clown's words.

But first there is Autolycus to contend with. His trick is cleverly carried out for he appeals to the clown's generous instincts. The pickpocketing occurs while the clown is being a good Christian. Autolycus is nearly caught out when the clown offers him money and has to be stopped from looking for his purse.

Having succeeded with his trick, Autolycus is happy to relish and embellish the joke by claiming that it was 'Autolycus' who robbed him, enjoying the clown's comments on that 'cowardly rogue' (108). Their exchange about courtly life has some bearing on the rest of the play. The clown assumes that virtue is cherished at Court, but Autolycus knows that 'vices' come in all guises, and he goes on to enumerate some of them (98–103). With warm words of gratitude Autolycus sends the clown off, then confides his roguish intentions to the audience.

Although the audience sympathises with the clown, Autolycus's villainies are thoroughly enjoyable, mainly because, through his candour, the audience is allowed to share his view of the world. He takes them into his confidence, addressing them more directly than any previous character except Time, the chorus. By this means Shakespeare has begun to shift the response to evil in the play. This shift is important in the pattern of the play as a whole. The world in which Autolycus's villainy operates is the countryside of Bohemia, which the scene has vividly evoked. Life in that countryside is closely connected with the cycle of the seasons. In that cycle Autolycus's crimes do not have a catastrophic effect. We can imagine a woman's horror at discovering the theft of a sheet she had put out to dry on a hedge in the sunshine (5–8), but it will not affect her future happiness disastrously. His reputation as described by the clown, suggests that his antics at 'wakes, fairs and bear-baiting' (105) have provided plenty of lively tales to offset the losses sustained by his victims. Even the theft of the clown's purse may be simply a story by next year's sheep-shearing festival. In fact, the theft is only mentioned once again in passing (IV.iv. 254–5), and certainly does not seem to spoil the pleasure of the feast in the first part of the next scene. Evil or vice, then, is to be present at the feast, but Polixenes in disguise will disrupt it more disastrously than Autolycus.

Act IV, scene iv

The scene is almost as long as Acts II and III put together, with many complications of plot. The action is continuous but it is best to discuss the scene in sections.

Summary
(a) 1–349
Florizel, disguised as a young countryman 'Doricles', praises Perdita, who is dressed up to be the Mistress of the Feast. She is apprehensive at his courtship, fearing the disapproval of his father, the king. Guests arrive for the feast, including Polixenes and Camillo in disguise, as well as the shepherds

and shepherdesses and the clown. The shepherd urges Perdita to welcome her guests, which she does, with appropriate flowers. The feast proceeds, with dances and the arrival of Autolycus, disguised as a pedlar. Polixenes questions the old shepherd about 'Doricles', whom the latter sees as a likely match for his daughter.

(b) 350-690

Polixenes disrupts the betrothal between Florizel and Perdita, revealing his true identity and Florizel's. He threatens the old shepherd with hanging, Florizel with being disinherited and Perdita with death. Camillo helps Florizel to flee with Perdita to the Sicilian Court but then goes to tell Polixenes. Autolycus becomes involved in the escape.

(c) 691-855

Autolycus stops the clown and shepherd reaching Polixenes to tell him about Perdita's true origins, luring them to board the ship bound for Sicilia.

Commentary

(a) 1-349

The first part of the scene introduces the characters of Florizel and Perdita and presents the sheep-shearing feast.

A striking feature of the scene as a whole is that all the major characters are in some form of disguise: Florizel, Polixenes, Camillo and Perdita, who is in double disguise. She is dressed up for the feast, and Florizel compares her to a queen or goddess. The audience knows that a queenly appearance reflects her status more truthfully than any character is aware. In her 'borrowed flaunts' (23), she is still not dressed as befits her royal birth. Florizel, too, is dressed more humbly than a prince, but Perdita can only see the difference between them. In the ensuing exchange each in their different ways shows both true and false judgement. Perdita dreads Polixenes's discovery of his son (18-24). She thinks Florizel's rank has made him over-optimistic and that his resolution to love her honourably will fail when Polixenes opposes it. Her fear of Polixenes is, of course, a correct prediction, but Florizel's resolution will turn out to be stronger than she realised. He compares himself to a god transformed for the sake of love. His belief in his own constancy is well-founded, but he is over-confident in anticipating no hindrance to their marriage. He urges her to 'darken not/The mirth o' the feast' (41-2). The scene proceeds with a slight shadow of the disaster to come.

From comparisons to gods and goddesses we move to the more earthly responsibilities of being a hostess. Perdita, who has already demonstrated her modesty, must now play the extrovert role her supposed father has given her, following in the footsteps of his wife. The shepherd paints a vivid picture of his wife bustling around, keeping her guests entertained and supplying them with food and drink. In one sense nothing could be a greater contrast to Perdita's true mother, the royal Hermione; yet the roles are similar in that Hermione too carried the responsibility for hospitality, and indeed it is towards the same man, Polixenes, that both Hermione and Perdita are urged to show a warm welcome.

Polixenes and Camillo, though strangers, are welcomed as honoured guests at the shepherds' feast. Perdita gives them appropriate flowers; Shakespeare's audience would have understood the language of flowers. Here, that language is developed into an intricate discussion between the young shepherdess and the older man, Perdita and Polixenes. This passage (77-103) does not advance the action and yet it is very important to the meaning of the play. First of all, it establishes their relationship and develops their characters. Both are courteous and respectful but hold to their own opinion. Perdita will not allow timidity or fear to let her swerve from what she thinks is the truth. Polixenes responds to her without any of the animosity he is to display later in the scene. Their disguises put them on a more equal footing than if they confronted each other openly as shepherdess and king. More significantly, the ideas that they express relate importantly to other ideas and themes in the play.

Polixenes compliments Perdita for choosing winter flowers to give to them, since they are suitable for older men. Perdita explains that it is now late summer when the prettiest flowers are carnations and pinks which are known as 'Nature's bastards'. She has grown none of them, she explains, because their stripes (piedness) are produced by art, not by 'great creating Nature' (86-8); Polixenes argues that nature makes art. In principle their debate is one that continues even now, the question being whether artificial scientific methods go against nature or whether man's inventive powers are simply part of the process of nature. The relationship between nature and art will be developed in the last act, when what appears to be art, the statue of Hermione, turns out to be nature, i.e. the real Hermione who lives and breathes.

Polixenes tries to persuade Perdita that the skill of grafting is good. He explains that the plant produced by cross-breeding a cultivated plant with a more common one, is actually an improvement on nature, but the skill that is used is natural. Perhaps enjoying his own eloquence, he seems totally oblivious to the fact that he is advocating a process for plants that he will not allow for human beings, though his argument depends logically on making human beings just as much part of nature as plants are. He talks about cross-breeding as 'we marry', yet we know he does *not* want his royal son, who could be considered 'a bud of nobler race', to be joined with Perdita, who, as a shepherdess, is 'of baser kind'.

Perdita acknowledges the rightness of his argument, but when he urges her therefore to cultivate gillyflowers, she still refuses. Unlike Polixenes she can see the link between her argument and her views on courtship:

the art used in creating these flowers is like that of women who wear make-up (an art not openly approved in Shakespeare's time). She would not like Florizel to wish to breed children by her because of a false appearance she presented. We are reminded of her modesty at the beginning of the scene, when she felt her robes were too showy for a 'lowly maiden'. Perdita's wholehearted distrust of changing one's appearance will not be borne out by the action of the scene, in which disguise will be used for both good and bad ends.

Turning to Florizel and the young shepherdesses, Perdita pours out words that conjure up the flowers of spring, equating them with love, beauty and marriage. Her mention of Greek gods and goddesses echoes Florizel's idyllic speech at the beginning of the scene. We may link Proserpina with Perdita herself, symbolising youth and springtime. And we may note that 'bright Phoebus' (114) is Apollo, already important in the play. By the end of the speech she expresses her love and desire for Florizel more openly than before.

Like the conversation with Polixenes, this speech advances the action hardly at all. At this point in the play, time stands still for a few moments. Florizel slows the action down even further, putting into words how much he relishes every single thing Perdita does, wanting her actions to go on for ever. Perdita's reply shows how closely truth and falsehood are bound up together at this point. She acknowledges Florizel's truth and honour in love, but addresses him by his false name, 'Doricles', and describes him untruthfully as an 'unstained shepherd'.

The stage action now splits. While the dance goes on, the audience gets enticing hints of how much the shepherd tells his guest, whom he thinks is an equal. But the conversation is cut off by the news of the pedlar's arrival.

The description of the pedlar and his wares evokes the country festivities: his ballads, his ribbons and tapes, his fabrics, Perdita's warning that he should not sing dirty songs, and his 'come-buy' song set a scene that would have been familiar to many of Shakespeare's audience. Mopsa and Dorcas quarrel over favours from the clown, showing a more down-to-earth comical view of courtship than Perdita's romantic speech. Their credulous reaction to the pedlar's (Autolycus's) exaggerated and unbelievable accounts of ballads adds comedy to the scene, and his tall stories give another variation on the theme of 'tales' in the play. The song is another form of home-grown entertainment typical of this feast.

Again, the conversation between the shepherd and Polixenes is cut off, this time by the announcement of another dance. This second dance is lustier and wilder than the first, with the herdsmen dancers dressed up in animal skins. The dance prevents the audience hearing the shepherd's words, which finally lead Polixenes to his resolution to part the young lovers. That decision pushes the action forward so significantly that the celebration of the feast is soon forgotten.

The sheep-shearing feast, then, has taken up most of the action in the scene so far, and created a kind of interlude for the audience. Shakespeare's portrayal of his pastoral scene is vivid, and takes on added vitality because its spirit of enjoyment and revelry is in such marked contrast to the rest of the play. Its characteristic quality is created by two different aspects of the pastoral world, for Shakespeare combines a realistic and an idealised view of the feast. The realistic aspects are expressed through speeches like the clown's in IV.iii (see page 27), the shepherd's speech encouraging Perdita (55–62) and the 'pedlar's' arrival. These are in prose, and capture the earthy, sometimes ribald quality of rustic life in Shakespeare's time. But at that period there was also a tendency among sophisticated people to idealise the virtues of simple, pastoral life, which people fondly imagined could provide an escape from the pressures and restraints of civilised life. This pastoral ideal was associated with the mythical times when gods and goddesses lived on the earth, or when, in Christian terms, the world was like a garden of Eden, untouched by evil. Florizel's speech at the beginning of the scene and Perdita's about the spring flowers depict that idealised world, which was a popular feature of romantic comedies in Shakespeare's time. Because this idyllic mood is conveyed by Florizel and Perdita, we associate it with their youth and love. Their youthfulness may remind us of Polixenes's memories of his boyhood in Act I. I have already linked his mention of 'shepherd's note' and 'lambs i' the sun' with this scene (see page 1). Now we see that his desire to be 'boy eternal' (see I.ii.65) is paralleled here by Florizel, who wants Perdita to dance 'ever' (IV.iv.140–3). Their love enhances their view of the world for each other, and by extension for other characters and for the audience. It also makes time stand still, and Shakespeare lets the audience share this sense of timelessness, by slowing down the events in this scene.

The combination of realism and idealisation is carried through in several ways: through the character of Perdita, who is both a shepherdess and a 'queen' in this scene; through the mixture of prose and verse; and through the interpenetration of the two views revealed in lines like those of the servant, who says that the pedlar sings over his wares 'as they were gods and goddesses' (211–12). The use of country songs and dances also contributes to the combined effect, the music lifting the tone of the scene, but still asserting its homespun quality.

The music alerts us to another aspect of the scene. Shakespeare does not depict an ordinary day among the shepherds, but a feast day, when they are performing a celebration. The whole scene functions as an interlude for the entertainment of the audience as well as for the characters. Song, dance, poetry, jokes and a simple story-line are combined in a way that would have been familiar to Shakespeare's audiences from the court masque (see page 3). This form of entertainment typically portrayed an idealised world of mythical characters, including abstract figures like Time, used earlier in the Act. Poetic debate was also a feature of the masques; the argument about flowers between Polixenes and Perdita is particularly appropriate because its topic, Nature and art, relates to the two aspects of the scene as a whole, the 'natural' and the 'artificial' view of rustic life.

Shakespeare incorporates the story line into his interlude through the presence of Polixenes and Camillo, threatening the joyous world of the lovers, even while centre stage is occupied with songs, dances and the tales of Autolycus. Now the moment comes for that threat to be revealed.

(b) 350-690

The second part of the scene has a clearer progression than the first part. The potential conflict between father and son is brought to a head, and then the action moves towards a reconciliation that embraces far more than the resolution of that conflict. The scene is complicated by the sheer *number* of forces that propel the events. Those forces express themselves through the characters, all of whose different actions, decisions and motives are necessary for the story to work out as it does. Power and control continually shift in this scene, as they did not under Leontes's tyranny in the first three Acts.

The first part of this section focuses on the father/son relationship. Polixenes does not at once carry out his decision to part the lovers. Instead he exploits the disguises further, to test Florizel's feeling. Florizel shows respect for the elderly guest he takes Polixenes to be, as well as love for Perdita, which he expresses in such high-flown language that Polixenes makes a joke about it (371-3). Then Florizel makes his public protestation in the widest terms he can find, calling on the whole universe to bear witness, naming all the qualities he can think of against which to measure the value of Perdita's love. There is some irony, since, though he is not the 'most imperial monarch' (378), yet he will wear a king's crown one day.

Polixenes's niggardly comment shows that the speech has offended him (384), Camillo's (385) gives Florizel credit for his feeling. The declaration precipitates the formal betrothal between 'Doricles' and Perdita. We note that the shepherd gives more attention to his daughter's wishes than many fathers would have done in Shakespeare's time. The key to Polixenes's anger is in Florizel's boast that 'One being dead/I shall have more than you can dream of yet' (394-5). Ironically, this phrase exactly parallels the shepherd, who had told Polixenes that Perdita would bring 'Doricles' 'That which he not dreams of' (181-2).

As Polixenes presses him, the irony is underlined by Florizel's continued courtesy to the 'guest' while stubbornly insisting on keeping his father in ignorance. It is not only the match itself which arouses Polixenes's anger, but his son's treatment of him. His first words are to disown the relationship which Florizel has so abused. Then he considers the unsuitability of the marriage, sketching a ludicrous picture of a king's son, who should be carrying a sceptre, carrying a sheephood instead (426-7). Compare with his pastoral references in I.ii: he finds the shepherds' world repellent when it comes to marriage.) His anger spreads to the shepherd and to Perdita with unreasoning haste, including some jealousy at his son's complete transfer of loyalty, as well as righteous indignation at Florizel's deceitfulness and unwise choice. It is on Perdita that the worst of his insults and threats fall (428-47). He leaves, but neither Camillo nor Florizel follows. Although Polixenes has utterly destroyed the happiness of the feast, the victims of his anger are not left alone as Hermione was.

The next part of the scene is a mixture of explanations and intricate arrangements. Polixenes's revelation and wrath, while bringing matters to a head, resolved nothing. The characters left on the stage are in disarray, in ignorance about each other's motives and intentions. But the powers for good in Perdita, Florizel and Camillo work towards clarity and firm purpose, which slowly lead to trust and positive action. Dramatically, much of the scene is an anticlimax, and like IV.ii can become tedious in performance. But the gradual unfolding of the events is necessary to the action. The audience must watch and listen patiently while the many threads are gathered together and the events move towards resolution.

The action depends first on Florizel and then on Camillo. Perdita's role is one of acceptance, first of defeat, then of trust in the plan devised by the other two. (Her character development is discussed on page 62) The shepherd retires, broken-hearted at his daughter's deceit, welcoming death. Florizel's simple words after the shepherd's speech (and presumably his exit) establish his position and release suspense: 'What I was, I am' (470). His constancy in love leads logically to his decision to escape. Declaiming his intentions to fulfil his oath, he measures his love on an even larger scale than before, not just against worldly prizes but against the whole earth and universe. (Compare his speeches 378-84 with 482-5 and 494-8.) And whereas in the earlier part of the scene such language might have been hyperbole (exaggeration for effect), here it is anchored to Florizel's real decision to disinherit himself and put to sea with Perdita. He prefers to be guided by his 'fancy' (488) and his 'senses' (490), not by reason alone. Florizel's passion, like Leontes', sweeps all before. Ironically his passionate love will put Perdita's life at risk just as Leontes's jealousy did. The crucial difference, of course, is that she is no longer to be abandoned.

Camillo now takes the initiative from Florizel, apparently switching his loyalty from father to son, just as he did from one king to another.

The next part of the scene is given over to Camillo's outline of his plan and his success in persuading Florizel to adopt it. He vividly imagines the scene of Florizel's arrival at Leontes's Court with his 'princess', fills in the details and even offers to write Florizel's script for him as a convincing embassy from Polixenes. Once he has won Florizel's trust, it remains simply to sort out the details of disguise: an appropriate moment for Shakespeare to bring Autolycus back.

As in his first entrance (IV.ii) Autolycus arrives on the stage with no clear intention. Scoffing at honesty and trust, he nevertheless confides in the audience very honestly about his *dishonesty*. When, a moment later, he discovers the presence of Camillo and the lovers, his self-congratulatory carefree mood switches in case they have overheard him. (His fear of hanging was well founded, since that was the punishment for thieves in Shakespeare's time.) But he is soon back in charge of the situation, playing victim again, and sniffing out some profit for himself.

Camillo makes Autolycus and Florizel exchange clothes. It is as well to check back over all the disguises, for exchange of garments is the main visual action in this section of the play. When did Florizel take off his 'Doricles' disguise? Perhaps as soon as his father took off *his* disguise. When did Perdita take off her festive costume? Perhaps when she said she would 'queen it no inch further' (455). If Camillo took off his when he addressed Florizel (472) that would have left all three in their true identity during this part where they made their plans (except for Perdita, known only to the audience.) Now at line 640, Florizel gives his Court clothes to Autolycus. Whether Autolycus still wears his pedlar's costume, or whether he is just in his rags, we note that Florizel does not recognise him as a former servant. Perdita covers her face and head to escape discovery. This whole piece of action is comical, with Camillo urging all of them to make haste, in view of the fact they have only just divested themselves of their former disguises. Florizel comments that his own father would not now recognise him, a grim joke considering the situation has arisen out of *his* non-recognition of his father. He takes Perdita aside, leaving Camillo free to tell the audience his true intention. Perhaps Shakespeare was consciously inviting the audience to laugh at the obviousness of his own dramatic devices here.

Camillo's direct contribution to the action is now drawing to an end. In arranging and even scripting the couple's arrival in Sicilia, his role has been like that of a playwright. The characters themselves acknowledge the theatricality of the situation. He tells Florizel he will have them dressed in royal robes 'as if/The scene you play were mine' (589–90). And when he makes Perdita muffle her appearance, she sees the situation as a play in which she must play a part. These references continue the idea of 'playing' that Shakespeare has already introduced. When we see Florizel and Perdita arrive at Leontes's court in the next Act, it will be as if we see Camillo's drama in production. Florizel, though, has other terms for Camillo. He calls him 'the preserver' of Polixenes and himself, and the 'medicine of our house' (592-3). These additions suggest a parallel with Paulina, the 'preserver' of the Sicilian house, and the 'medicine' that Leontes needed.

There are also parallels between Autolycus and Camillo. Both are pragmatists, finding possibilities in the immediate situation for furthering their own aims. But where Autolycus is motivated by self-interest, Camillo bases his actions on true loyalty and service.

Autolycus's decision at this point is to be dishonest, because by that means he will be 'constant to my profession' (690). His words about honesty and constancy seem trifling, but they reflect the complications of honesty and constancy in the behaviour of both Camillo and Florizel in this scene. We should note also his sharp awareness of the present time, talking of 'this time of lethargy' (620-1), 'this is the time that the unjust man doth thrive' (680-1) and 'the gods do this year connive at us' (683-4). These remarks make us conscious of the other characters caught in the timespan of the play, whose actions, like his, may or may not be punished or rewarded. At this point, many questions still hang over the outcome of the story.

(c) 691-855

One piece of this jigsaw puzzle of a plot has yet to be fitted in: the secret of Perdita's origins, known only to the audience, must be revealed, for the plot to achieve the inevitable resolution we expect from this romantic tale. In this last part of the scene, through Autolycus's tricks and manoeuvres, the key to that secret is carried to Sicilia, as the shepherd and clown are brought to Florizel's ship, bearing their precious evidence with them.

The audience is now given a broader piece of comedy to round off the Bohemian scenes, with the three characters first encountered there. The scene presents a contrast between the simple honesty of the shepherd and the clown, and Autolycus's trickery. Autolycus is in control. As he teases the two men, with his satirical impression of a court official, Autolycus is playing for time, while he decides whether to help or hinder their quest to see the king (as perhaps Shakespeare is too, in keeping the audience in comic suspense instead of pushing quickly through to the last act). Autolycus's close questioning and the emphasis on social position makes the exchange comically relevant to Perdita's situation, culminating in Autolycus's satirical reference to their simple nature (758-60), lines which are like a parody of the earlier discussion of nature, breeding and social rank. The scene is stretched out with variations of Autolycus's prevarications until he alights on the idea of inventing imagined tortures for the shepherd and his son, whom he has pretended not to recognise, and who dare not confess their identity. The punishments he improvises are a rich parody of the worst that Polixenes or Leontes could ever have dreamed up.

This leisurely, drawn-out, comical end to the Act fittingly completes the summer scenes in the Bohemian countryside. Though this long scene has been a contrast to the Sicilian scenes in mood, characters' decisions have brought the play ever closer to the Sicilian Court again. Some of the action is parallel to the action of Act I: Polixenes's anger and Florizel's passion and unswerving purpose are like Leontes's, Camillo is put into a position not unlike his predicament in Act I. And Perdita is put to sea as she was in Act III. But the similarities themselves allow us to see how much less wintry and severe has been the action in the sunnier, gentler climes of Bohemia. Everyone threatened by Polixenes's anger is escaping it, Florizel's passion and purpose are born, not of jealousy, but of deep love and admiration; Camillo's advice and double-dealing are leading towards reconciliation, not painful separation; and Autolycus's tricks are so light-hearted that they are just as likely to lead to good as evil.

Act V, scene i

Summary
At the Sicilian court, Leontes, still lamenting the wrongs he did, promises Paulina he will not remarry except at her bidding, despite his courtiers' protests. Florizel and his 'princess' arrive, but their plan is foiled by the announcement of Polixenes's arrival with Camillo. Florizel persuades Leontes to act as an intermediary with Polixenes.

Commentary
In this scene the audience is in a powerful situation of knowledge, able to predict the events and watch them unfold.

Leontes's penitence is as Polixenes described it in IV.ii. He laments afresh the deaths of Hermione and Mamillius, carrying out the vow he made in III.iii.238–43. He is like the character in Mamillius's tale for winter, a man dwelling by a churchyard (II.i.25–31). Around him an argument is waged between Paulina, who keeps Leontes's mind on the past, and the courtiers who want him to look to the future, and especially to secure an heir to the throne. As in Acts II and III, the male courtiers disapprove of Paulina's insistence that he confront his wrong. Cleomenes and Dion talk of 'present comfort' and 'future good', and even though they are the very men who received the oracle of Apollo, they are prepared to go against its instruction, against what Paulina calls the 'secret purposes' of the gods. She tells Leontes to 'care not for issue' (46) her words having that double meaning attached before: she is advising him let the gods take care of future events and provide an heir.

Audience sympathy is precariously balanced between Paulina and the courtiers. Leontes's life is impotent and painful, his submission to Paulina complete. But she is the guardian of the oracle's truth. Leontes easily accepts the idea of having no wife, conjuring up a picture of Hermione's ghost reproaching him so much that he would murder his new wife. Note his tendency, still, to visualise horrific situations. Far from soothing him over these painful imaginings, Paulina encourages him, even embellishing the picture so vividly that to him it becomes a confused vision of stars, eyes and coal. (67-8). From this nightmare she has actually helped to create, Paulina extracts his oath not to seek a wife. In the conditions of this oath her words become most mysterious, as she drops hints like an oracle herself. With her hints about 'another/As like to Hermione as is her picture' (73-5) and a queen whom Hermione's ghost would enjoy seeing him embrace (78-81), Paulina's words mean nothing to the other characters and confuse the audience who can interpret them either as ironic references to Perdita's arrival, or as veiled references to Hermione's existence. Leontes, unable to understand any of her implications, simply repeats his promise not to marry without her permission. Then she says it will never be until Hermione is alive again. This simple prophecy seems as unlikely to be fulfilled as Apollo's, which she herself had said was 'monstrous to our human reason'. At the point when Florizel's arrival is announced, Leontes's oath is the only event that has furthered the action of the scene, and Paulina's hints and prophecy the only words that were not clear and predictable for the audience.

From the announcement of Florizel's arrival, to the announcement of Polixenes's, the action is an enactment of Camillo's plans, the staging, if you like, of his drama. But the scene is not lacking in dramatic tension. Suspense is created over the success of the plan: how well will Florizel and Perdita play their parts, convincing Leontes and the Court they are truly a royal embassy from Polixenes? The effect of their arrival on Leontes and the rest of the court is also significant, an effect which, as we have seen, Camillo could only sketchily imagine (IV.iv.553-60).

Before Leontes receives the couple, the mother/daughter parallel between Hermione and Perdita is emphasised for the audience. The gentleman describes Florizel's princess in quite ecstatic terms (94-5) causing Paulina to reproach him for forgetting Hermione. Paulina also draws the parallel between Florizel and Mamillius, who were the same age. As when she talked of Hermione's death, Leontes's first response is to resist the pain this comparison causes him, but he then allows himself to confront it, as the couple enter.

Shakespeare thus prepares the audience to appreciate to the full the impact of Florizel and Perdita on Leontes. Camillo foresaw that Florizel would be a visual reminder to him of Polixenes. Now, the parallel with

Mamillius has been introduced, together with that between Hermione and Perdita. What in fact has the most powerful impact on Leontes is Florizel's similarity to the young Polixenes. A moment before, he had feared that the sight of Florizel would make him lose his reason. Now that sight conjures up youthful memories of wild deeds, a happier kind of madness than the painful association with Mamillius. Turning to Perdita, he immediately praises her even more highly than the gentleman had done. Then he speaks of the 'couple' he has lost who might have stood there as they do. Here the double meanings converge. Which couple does he mean? Does Florizel still stand for Polixenes, and is he coupled with the memory of Hermione, as they stood in Act I? Or does Florizel now change in Leontes's mind to represent Mamillius, and Florizel's princess represent Leontes's other lost child, whom the audience knows she really is? At this moment all the references Shakespeare has introduced about children being 'copies' of their parents, are realised as Leontes gazes at Florizel and Perdita. The point is also made that people can be 'lost' in several ways, through death and through loss of youth, as well as through separation, discord and ignorance.

The first positive effect of seeing Florizel is that Leontes discovers something new to live for: he wants to see Polixenes again. The audience knows that he very soon will see his friend again, but also knows that that is the last thing Florizel wants. Florizel's set speech gives Polixenes's infirmity from old age as the reason for sending his son (a somewhat tactless excuse for Camillo to have thought of). Moved by the assurance of Polixenes's love, and trained by Paulina to be quickly reminded of his wrongs, Leontes feels them stir again and reproaches himself for his treatment of Polixenes. This raises our sympathy for Leontes, knowing that in fact he is overrating the affection of Polixenes, who will come in pursuit of his son, not of his friend.

Leontes turns to Perdita. His comment on the discomfort of the sea voyage together with Florizel's eloquent description of the supposed heartfelt parting between the 'princess' and her noble father in Libya, underlines for the audience the unfatherly treatment Leontes has given this same princess. Entirely convinced by Florizel's false speech, Leontes calls blessings down on their stay in Sicilia. He believes that his own childless state is the punishment of heaven for his wrong against Polixenes; and conversely that heaven has rewarded Polixenes's goodness with a son. Shakespeare underlines the irony again as Leontes regrets not having a son and daughter of his own. His words also emphasise his false judgement of how heaven punishes and rewards. No relationship has yet been established between Leontes and Perdita, for he has not addressed her directly and she has not spoken at all, presumably contending with the daunting task of hiding her identity of shepherdess under her royal robes.

With the news of Polixenes's arrival, the audience sees Camillo's plans continue to be implemented, while Florizel's and Perdita's hopes are temporarily shattered. Leontes is thrust into the swift passage of events, and must make active decisions as a king rather than trust Paulina to make them for him.

The relationship between Florizel and Leontes now becomes crucial. For the first time in the play, Leontes's response is healthily balanced between reason and passion: he sides with Polixenes but sympathises with Florizel's predicament. Florizel also balances qualities that were at war in him before: he comforts Perdita, reminding her of the constancy of their love, and he humbly asks Leontes's help as an advocate, whereas in Act IV he has steadfastly refused to be honest or respectful towards his father. He acknowledges their common ground: Leontes was young once and therefore experienced affection. Leontes, too, finds the common ground, expressing his admiration of Perdita so flirtatiously that Paulina reprimands him as she had done the gentleman, comparing Perdita unfavourably with Hermione. Where remembrance of Hermione had brought him nothing but pain before, now it prompts him to take action on behalf of the young couple. Shakespeare shows us here an unselfish Leontes, bent on reconciling father and son, and on fulfilling Florizel's desires, *before* he learns of Perdita's true identity.

An aspect of the scene that needs further examination is the characters' frequent references to heaven, the gods and other associated religious language. The opening speech has 'saint-like', 'redeemed', 'penitence', 'trespass', 'the heavens', and 'forgive', all of which relate closely to Christianity, but references to Apollo's oracle also occur. The characters often guess wrongly how they stand in the eyes of the 'heavens'. Paulina insists on Leontes's celibacy because she does not realise that the last part of Apollo's oracle is being fulfilled. Leontes asks the 'blessed gods' to purify Sicilia while Florizel and his princess are there, assuming that Sicilia is still infected with his evil. Perdita thinks the heavens are against her marriage. In all these instances the heavens' forgiveness and the purifying of Sicilia are much nearer than the characters recognise, being represented by the presence of Perdita. Significantly though, the characters do associate her with the gods, first when she is compared with the foundress of a religion (106-9) and then when Leontes calls her a goddess (130).

One more language reference may clarify the significance of this scene. In his second speech to Florizel, Leontes feels the wrongs he has done to Polixenes stirring 'afresh' (148). Three lines later, he says Florizel is welcome 'As is the spring to th'earth' (151). Leontes has spent sixteen years lamenting his wrongs 'afresh'. It is easy to see how Perdita and Florizel represent the youthful renewing vigour of spring, but not so easy to

accept that Leontes, renewing his penitence all that time, has also con-
tributed to the springtime that has come to Sicilia after the long winter
he imposed on it. Yet the evidence is in the scene, for as the action has
shown, the *freshness* of his sense of the wrong he did Polixenes leads him
to agree to Florizel's request, seeking a reconciliation that will permit
the marriage of Florizel and Perdita, which we know will bring youth and
hope of fruitfulness both to Bohemia and to Sicilia.

Act V, scene ii

Summary

Three Gentlemen, together with Autolycus, exchange news about the
reunions between Leontes, Camillo and Polixenes, the discovery that
Perdita is Leontes's lost heir and the plan to visit the statue of Hermione.
Autolycus comments on his own part in the discovery. The shepherd and
the clown, now elevated to being 'gentlemen', enjoy their new status.

Commentary

This comical scene may take the audience by surprise. Instead of seeing
the action brought to the happy conclusion they have anticipated, the
audience sees the events recounted by minor characters, none of the major
characters being present on the stage. This indirect treatment of the
action has several important effects. First it changes the audience's position
in relation to the story. For all the action since the discovery of the baby,
the audience has enjoyed superior knowledge but here they are placed
in the same position as the courtiers who have been 'commanded out of
the chamber' (6). This treatment elevates and distances the principal
characters. Another important effect is the lightening of tone in the
Sicilian Court. The narrations may raise a smile, and by his presentation
of the shepherd and the clown Shakespeare links the comic tone associated
with the scenes in Bohemia, with the seriousness of the Sicilian scenes. A
third effect of this treatment is that it provides dramatic relief before the
true climax of the last scene. Instead of piling revelation upon revelation,
thus reducing the impact of each, Shakespeare inserts a more humdrum
scene here as a contrast to the final, most important revelation, which can
therefore make its full dramatic effect.

The use of prose alerts us to the informal nature of the scene. Through
the narrations there is a contrast between the ordinariness of the courtiers
and the extraordinariness of the events they tell. The first gentleman
admits not only his limited knowledge but his inadequacy in recounting
it. What he did witness of the reunion was so astonishing that his account
of it is indeed garbled. He cannot decide if Leontes and Camillo were
expressing joy or sorrow. As he tries to explain how they were themselves
bereft of words, he stumbles into a kind of eloquence himself, saying

that there was 'speech in their dumbness, language in their very gestures'.
So joy and sorrow, comic and serious are combined both in *what* he
describes and *how* he describes it.

This mingling of joy and sorrow continues. Shakespeare gently parodies
the self-importance of the third gentleman who prides himself both on
knowing everything and on describing it. His account fills all the gaps in
the story, even telling them about what happened to Antigonus. The telling
is so swift that it may be comic in itself, like watching a film that has been
speeded up. He sums up the mixture of joy and sorrow in Paulina, with
words that depict a quite ludicrous picture: 'She had one eye declined
for the loss of her husband, another elevated that the oracle was fulfilled'
(80-2). Yet the first gentleman immediately comments on the 'dignity of
this act' (86). As in the original account of Antigonus's death, Shakespeare
holds a balance between laughter and tears. The last part of the third
gentleman's tale describes Perdita's emotion at hearing the story of her
mother, expressing that most movingly.

Through the gentlemen's eagerness to know and tell what has been
happening, and their impatience to see the statue, and through the emphasis
on the wonder of the events, Shakespeare invites us to consider what makes
us believe or disbelieve in the truth of events. In this scene he juggles with
the different ways we seek and confirm our knowledge, if not by seeing
for ourselves, then by eye-witness accounts which may convince us even
of what seems unbelievable.

Autolycus lacks that eagerness to know. He cares only how well he can
serve his own needs. So he does not follow the gentlemen off, but stays
to consider his opportunity of advancement, lost simply through Florizel's
and Perdita's seasickness. The audience is thus informed as to why the
lovers were still in ignorance about Perdita's origins when they arrived at
Leontes's court. The very absurdity of the explanation is perhaps a parody
on the twists and turns of the plot.

In the second part of this scene, the tables are turned on Autolycus.
The shepherd and the clown come on, dressed up to suit their newly-acquired
status. Good humour reigns. The comedy centres first on the clown's
insistence that he is not only a 'gentleman' but a 'gentleman born', since
four hours ago; then on the complicated relationships between these
two and the royal families; then on the clown's determination to behave
in an appropriately gentlemanly way, by nobly forgiving Autolycus his
misdeeds and swearing he is honest. The whole question of social equality
is comically resolved by their elevation. Remembering the debate on
breeding flowers, we may note that Perdita herself has turned out to be
'pied', and of mixed origins, combining in herself both base and noble
social origins. The shepherd is naïvely conscious of the qualities of gentleness and honesty that should go with being a gentleman. Yet is is because

he and the clown were born with those characteristics, that they cared for Perdita and preserved her. Their present status comes about because they were, in the truest sense, 'gentlemen born'. Autolycus plays up to their simple concerns, probably suspecting that he will be able to take advantage of the 'good masters' they promise to be.

In this scene then, the important events have been dealt with indirectly. In the same way, some of the important ideas in the play are referred to by touches in the language, of which the characters may be unaware, but which enrich the associations of the scene. For example the word 'issue', the third gentleman's use of the word 'pregnant' (33), 'angled' (90), recalling Leontes's and Polixenes's use of that word, and 'marble' which 'changed colour' (97-8) which anticipates the last scene. Autolycus refers to the clothes of the shepherd and the clown as 'the blossoms of their fortune' (134-5) recalling the flowers of the feast and their discovery of the baby, whom Antigonus had laid down with the words 'Blossom, speed thou well!' (III.iii.46).

At the end of the scene all the characters in it leave the stage to see the queen's statue. All the plot ends seem to have been tied up. Yet there is a sense of anticipation and suspense as the audience waits to see if there is anything else to be revealed.

Act V, scene iii

Summary

The two kings and their children, together with Camillo and other courtiers, are brought by Paulina to the chapel in her house to see the statue of Hermione. All are impressed at how lifelike it is. Paulina says she can make it move if Leontes wishes, calls for music, and urges the statue to come to life. Hermione descends from the pedestal, a living woman, and is reunited with Leontes and Perdita. Leontes presents Camillo to Paulina as a husband, asks pardon of Hermione and Polixenes and tells Hermione of Florizel's betrothal to Perdita. Then he leads everyone away to recount all that has happened.

Commentary

In this last scene the audience is asked to accept the most incredible part of the whole story, the coming to life of Hermione after sixteen years. How far they do accept it will vary from one member of the audience to another. What we can do here is to trace the features in the scene which may lead the audience towards suspending disbelief and sharing the sense of wonder that the characters experience.

Throughout most of the scene Paulina controls the action. It is her drama just as the trial scene was Leontes's, and Florizel's arrival in Sicilia was Camillo's.

The first twenty lines are an exchange between Leontes and Paulina which establishes a slow and serious mood. Leontes expresses his gratitude to Paulina and she acknowledges him gracefully for being her guest. Since these words are spoken in front of others, they take on an air of ceremonial between the King and his hostess. The setting, in a chapel, also gives an air of solemnity and mystery, which the audience may feel privileged to witness after the second-hand experience of the previous scene. Paulina prepares them to see something remarkable. She tells them she keeps the statue 'lonely and apart', so that when she says 'But here it is' (18), they will feel privileged to be allowed to see it and the audience shares that sense of special favour. They will see life 'mocked' as closely as sleep mocks death: the mingling of these terms – life, sleep, death, art – puts many impressions in the audience's minds at the very moment when she draws the curtain back to reveal the statue. Is it a statue or is it the dead Hermione? Is it, indeed, the living Hermione? In theatrical terms, is it a theatrical prop or a real actor? In performance, the actress playing the part must stand perfectly still for over eighty lines (20-103); life must mock art. That in itself is impressive, so the audience may admire for a number of reasons, either because they have been taken in as much as the characters, thinking they see a life-like statue, or because they see statue-like life. The characters stand in admiring silence, looking like statues themselves. The audience has already once before in Act III seen Hermione standing still with all the Court's eyes upon her, defending her life and honour and 'mocking' death when she swooned at the end of her trial. The moment may also recall the 'mock' queen, Perdita, when she stood at the feast, with her flowers, and Florizel gazed at her in admiration.

There are several moments when the secret of the statue is almost revealed before Paulina wishes, but she allays suspicion each time. The first is when she praises the artist for adding sixteen years to Hermione's appearance (30-2), the second is when she prevents Perdita from kissing the statue's hand (47-9), the third may be when she starts to draw the curtain (59) perhaps afraid Leontes has seen the 'statue' move. Certainly Leontes's next lines emphasise qualities of life – breath, flowing blood and moving eyes – but Paulina suggests it is his excitement that makes him think it lives. She is skilfully using Leontes's disturbed state of mind to make him think his imagination and wishful thinking are playing tricks on him (60-1, 69-70). His deep emotion has been shown not only in the comments of the other characters but in his obsession with the 'stone' (24-7, 34-8). Its coldness and stillness contrast with the warmth and tenderness he associates with Hermione, and reproach him for his treatment of her.

Having witnessed Leontes's wonder over the statue and the grief it aroused in him, Paulina recognises that he does want to think Hermione is alive, even though that is painful. She has also, by this time, given Hermione ample apportunity to witness the depth and sincerity of Leontes's penitence. She offers to 'afflict' him further and he welcomes that affliction as being sweet as 'any cordial comfort' (77). As in III.ii and V.i, Paulina recognises, as the other characters do not, the remedial power of Leontes's pain and grief.

Leontes is now standing so close to the statue that he sees its breath, though he still believes it is just his imagination and that if he kisses it the others may mock him. Yet again the suspense is tightened, but still Paulina prevents the discovery of Hermione. She insists that the paint is wet and wants to draw the curtain again. When Leontes and Perdita protest, Paulina offers those present the possibility of further amazement, but she puts the responsibility of choice on them. She disclaims the use of black magic, and when she has Leontes's consent, tells him that this act depends on an act of faith on the part of everyone there. Her dismissal of anyone who thinks it is unlawful also emphasises that the co-operation of the characters is needed. The audience may count themselves among those present, needing to waken their own faith in the events they are watching.

When Leontes says he is content with whatever Paulina will have the statue do, he repeats the word 'content' showing he is now ready to forgive himself, for otherwise the pain of having Hermione speak to him would be too great to bear. He bids Paulina to go on: 'Proceed/No foot shall stir'. The characters and the audience are now quite still, and it will be Hermione who moves. Paulina calls for music, which gives the moment a ritualistic quality. The scene is, after all, in a chapel, so that what occurs is like a religious ceremony, which is turned, at least for the characters, into a miracle. Paulina's words, spoken as the music plays, are like an incantation. The suspense is drawn out again, for it takes five lines before Hermione's stirring is perceivable (99–104) and someone, probably Leontes, starts in response to her movement. Paulina guides the action still, making Leontes offer his hand to Hermione in response to hers, which has been stretched out to him in what he already called 'her natural posture' (23) in which she stood when he first wooed her.

Still the characters are unsure how to explain what is happening. '*If this be magic*', Leontes says (110) but a moment later Camillo says '*If she pertains to life*', and Polixenes wants to know either where she has lived, or how she has returned from the dead. Paulina teases their credulousness, and by extension the audience's, saying that if it were a tale (which of course it is to the audience) people would hoot in disbelief. She allows that Hermione appears to live, and brings Perdita to her mother, to get her to speak. The final proof that Hermione lives is to be her speaking, partly because she will presumably give some explanation. But Hermione passes swiftly over what has happened to her, without giving any plausible story. After calling the gods to bless her daughter, she wants to know *her* story, and gives short shrift to her own. She has 'preserved' herself because Paulina said the oracle gave hope that Perdita was alive. This does not even make complete sense, since Hermione was present when the oracle was read. Only Hermione and Paulina share the secret of whether she 'really' died and came back to life.

Paulina prevents any further explanations and sends them all away, her own part in the story completed, as she thinks. But Leontes, restored to the dignity and responsibility of his position, takes it upon himself to bring the scene to an end. Paulina's description of herself as an 'old turtle' did not, of course, raise the laugh that it does nowadays, since it was short for 'turtle dove'. (Remember that Florizel took Perdita's hand with the same word on his lips at IV.iv.154.) Nevertheless the tone does lighten as the king decides to pair Paulina and Camillo. This match between his two loyal servants shows us he can now think beyond his own welfare.

That done, he has two more tasks to perform swiftly here before the action is complete. We note that there is apparently some tentativeness in the reunion between Polixenes and Hermione, for Leontes has to urge her to look upon his brother and then begs their pardon for his 'ill suspicion'. Lastly, he presents Florizel to her, indicating the double connection that will bind the two royal families closer than before. The reunion and reconciliation have been rapidly completed, but only in outline. Leontes recognises the need to go over all the events more slowly. Speed and slowness are combined in these last lines, as he speaks of how they will exchange their parts in the story 'leisurely' (152), but demands that they go off to do it 'Hastily' (155). Perhaps the rapid pace he precipitated in Acts I–III will now be combined with the slower rhythm of the pastoral scenes.

The final scene has presented a happier conclusion than any of the characters imagined. Almost all the pain that has been inflicted is now turned into joy. Leontes's worst crime is cancelled, for Hermione is alive. Antigonus died, it is true, but the marriage between Paulina and Camillo must compensate for that. No one mentions Mamillius, the other innocent victim sacrificed: the union between Perdita and Florizel must compensate for his death.

The main achievement of the scene is the concentration of so many ideas in the play into the one extraordinary moment when the 'statue' stirs. That moment contains the 'secret' of life in a physical and literal sense. It emphasises the difference between life and death, and between life and art, in the most basic way. Something that breathes, is warm, moves, and speaks, is neither dead nor stone but a living being, subject to time and passion.

There are three possible explanations for what has happened. One explanation is that Hermione at the end is a statue come to life. This requires the same kind of belief as for a fairy story. It is easy to imagine this form of the story being told by ballad makers through Sicilia and Bohemia, for the entertainment of people like Mopsa and Dorcas.

Another explanation is that Hermione died and was brought back to life again at some point during the sixteen years. This requires religious faith, which allows for miracles to happen at the wishes of some divine power, to fulfil some divine purpose. The amount of religious language in the play gives much weight to this explanation, especially the oracle and the emphasis on forgiveness.

The third explanation, that Hermione simply shut herself away for sixteen years with the connivance of Paulina, depends only on natural forces, that is, the passing of time and the performing of human actions. Yet it requires as much, if not more faith than the other two explanations.

3 THEMES

What is *The Winter's Tale* about? What is its meaning? A play communicates moment by moment, through its language, plot, structure, characters, stagecraft and style. Much of what can be said about the meaning of *The Winter's Tale* has already been indicated in the 'summaries and commentary' and will be referred to in the 'technical features'. However, it is helpful to pick out some of the themes, i.e. the recurrent ideas that give meaning to the play as a whole.

The overall sweep of the play is from *evil* and *discord* to *reconciliation, forgiveness, restoration* and *harmony.* The play hinges on Leontes's jealousy, its evil consequences and the happiness that is nevertheless restored through the preservation and discovery of Perdita and Hermione's return to life. Shakespeare also deals with the forces behind these events, in particular the processes of nature and time, and the idea of divine knowledge. Let us look briefly at each of these main themes and also at the way they might be linked together.

3.1 LEONTES'S JEALOUSY AND ITS CONSEQUENCES

Leontes's passionate jealousy begins very early in the play. In the Commentary to I.ii I examined how it began and showed how quickly it develops, leading to dire consequences. These consequences, presented through the rest of I, II and part of III, include hatred, injustice, death, loss of friends and family, and separation.

The beginning and development of Leontes's jealousy brings out questions about human relationships. For example, the sudden change of heart towards his wife and friend shows inconstancy in his affection. His accusation that Hermione's manner is 'too warm' shows that he is making judgments (or rather misjudgments) about what is the appropriate level of warmth and coldness in behaviour, it also relates to the question of hospitality towards Polixenes. And his quick suspicion of his childhood friend suggests an underlying rivalry in their relationship.

Leontes's jealousy quickly leads to *tyranny* in two senses: first, the tyranny that his passion and delusion have over his mind and heart, so that he can neither see nor feel nor think of anything else, and bases all his actions on the jealous delusion. This delusion is likened to a disease which needs medicine. The tyranny that he exerts over others leads to terrible consequences of cruelty, death, loss and separation. It also brings into the play the theme of *loyalty* and *obedience,* as his servants have to choose whether to obey him blindly out of fear, or seek another way of showing their loyalty.

Leontes's delusion leaves him even more suddenly than it overtook him. He sees his injustice, ceases to be tyrannical and begins his long penitence, guided by Paulina, who had sought all along to be his cure.

At that point in the play, Shakespeare leaves Leontes, but it is typical of his art that some of the themes underlying his treatment of Leontes's jealousy continue in the later parts of the play. For example, Polixenes's tyrannical behaviour parallels Leontes's, and leads to some of the same consequences, though not so disastrously; Florizel's constancy in love is an important contrast to Leontes's sudden change against his wife. The question of loyalty and obedience is reopened through Camillo's dilemma, and made fun of through the character of Autolycus. Camillo parallels Paulina in being the medicine of his master.

3.2 LOSS AND DISCOVERY – PERDITA'S DOUBLE IDENTITY

The loss of Perdita is a direct consequence of Leontes's jealous rage (though he actually intended her death.) So from the moment that she makes her appearance as a baby, her survival (through the good nature of Antigonus and the old shepherd) is a good event to set against the evil caused by Leontes.

It is important to remember that she is actually found several times over. The first time, her life is saved but her true identity remains lost. Florizel's discovery of her awakens their love, Polixenes's the threat to that love. The last time she is discovered, the secret of who she really is is revealed, though not in front of the audience. Through all these discoveries, she becomes the instrument of *reconcilation* between the two kings. And the truth of the oracle is proved: 'The King shall live without an heir if that which is lost be not found'.

Perdita's double identity as both shepherdess and unrecognised princess brings out some new themes in the play. The first is the theme of *social rank*, which is also carried through the comedy around the characters of the old shepherd and clown. Perdita is brought up as a shepherd's daughter, then restored to her birthright as a princess. In Shakespeare's time the difference between higher and lower classes was greater than in modern Birtain. Most people believed, as the clown and old shepherd seem to, that the higher classes had special qualities of breeding, nobility, courtesy and gentleness, but Shakespeare turns that attitude topsy turvy. Perdita has those qualities, but it is arguable whether it is because she was born a princess (for Leontes certainly abuses them, and so does Polixenes, both kings.) Rather, she has learnt them through the kind and virtuous treatment, though uncouth, that she has had from her supposed 'father' and 'brother'. It is not inborn breeding, but upbringing that has shaped her character. And yet both Polixenes and Camillo think that she seems to be better than her fellow-countrypeople. Thus Shakespeare leaves the matter unresolved but pursues it comically through Autolycus's teasing of the old shepherd and clown about courtly behaviour.

The old shepherd and clown assume that these qualities of nobility, gentleness and courtesy are not only a matter of social rank, but that they have a great deal to do with dress and manner. Their attitude relates to another aspect of the same theme - the question of *appearance* and *truth*. Perdita herself puts forward an argument against disguise and artifice which conceals the truth or falsifies nature. But the action of the play and her own concealed identity contradicts some of her arguments (see Commentary on IV.iv).

There is another element in Perdita's double identity, and that is the parallel between Hermione and her, which is brought out several times in IV.iv and V.i. She herself is like a resurrection of Hermione, foreshadowing the later resurrection.

3.3 THE RESURRECTION OF HERMIONE

The coming to life of the statue is a culmination of many of the themes of the play. As we have seen, she has already been brought to life in a sense through the growth of Perdita. The incident also extends the theme of appearance and truth.

Most importantly, Hermione's resurrection represents the triumph of *nature over art, good over evil* and *life over death*.

Nature and art have been treated earlier in the play, most specifically through Polixenes's and Perdita's debate (IV.iv) in which Polixenes argues that 'great creating Nature' is like an artist herself. The idea of nature making copies of her work, like an artist, i.e. children, has been touched on several times, through the parallels between Mamillius, Perdita and Florizel and their parents, Hermione and Leontes, and Polixenes.

To Leontes, Hermione's return to life is something more miraculous than nature's art, for nature herself could not bring the dead back to life. Hermione is most emphatically herself, sixteen years older. That seems to him the triumph of life over death. Although there is a plausible explanation, i.e. that Hermione did not in fact die, and her preservation has been foreshadowed through Perdita, the effect of having her living and breathing is like a miracle of resurrection which has come about through forgiveness. The importance of forgiveness has been prepared for in V.i, when Leontes, having repented for sixteen years, still cannot forgive himself for the wrongs he did. Hermione is the sign that he *is* forgiven. She is the instrument of forgiveness which has been granted to him because he has repented and because Perdita was found. By the end of the play, *good* has redeemed *evil*.

3.4 TIME AND THE SEASONS

The importance of the seasons is brought out first by the title, then by the heartening effect of the summer festival in IV. It is tempting to try to put 'seasons' to each part of the play, but such a clear pattern does not seem to have been Shakespeare's intention. Rather, the cycle of seasons is something against which to parallel the cycle of human life. Spring parallels youth, and new life; winter is old, cold, cruel, dead and buried. Through this parallel Shakespeare is able to show that the passing of sixteen years in human life is long enough for a new generation to be born, in the same way that new plants grow up and flourish in a half-cycle of the seasons.

The theme of time and the seasons does not relate to any one incident of the play, but is touched on many times, notably in I.ii and IV. It helps to show that, although Leontes's wrongs seem to dominate everything, the forces of time and nature are beyond human power and push life through a cycle of birth, growth, decay, death and regeneration which no man can stop. However deep a winter Leontes created in Sicilia, spring, personified by Perdita and Florizel, does come. The title of the story on which Shakespeare based the play was *The Triumph of Time*.

3.5 THE ORACLE AND ITS FULFILMENT

Apollo's Oracle is important in the play because it represents the theme of *divine power*, though there are also important references to Christianity (see p.70). It reveals the truth about the past (Hermione has not been unfaithful), the present (Leontes is a jealous tyrant) and correctly prophesies the future (the king does live without an heir until Perdita is found). Thus, divine power is represented as divine knowledge. Leontes's final crime is to reject that knowledge. The theme of *knowledge* is important throughout the play and is linked with *belief* (e.g. Leontes believes Hermione is guilty, the other characters believe she is innocent) and *superstition* (e.g. the old shepherd thinks Perdita was left by the fairies).

There are a few moments when divine power seems to affect the action of the play, e.g. Mamillius's death, which Leontes sees as Apollo's punishment for rejecting the oracle, and the storm, which Antigonus interprets as Apollo's anger. These are moments when the characters interpret divine power as best they can. They may be simply chance occurrences, just as the recovery of Perdita and her meeting with Florizel may be. But it is also possible to interpret them as part of a divine pattern leading to the reconciliation at the end.

Another way in which Shakespeare brings in the theme of divine power is by comparing his characters with gods, especially Florizel and Perdita (see Commentary on IV.iv and V.i). These comparisons, together with the links with the story of Christ, hint at the possibility of gods appearing on earth and prepare for the religious atmosphere of the last scene.

3.6   HUMAN LIFE AS A DRAMA – AN OVERVIEW OF THE PLAY

You have seen that many of the themes of the play connect and overlap, e.g. a conflict between *inner truth* and *outward appearance* occurs over Leontes's misunderstanding of what he sees between Polixenes and Hermione (his delusion), over Perdita's 'false' identity, and over the 'statute' which is not a statue. It is important to connect any theme that you are asked to consider to the main topics outlined above. You are not likely, in studying the play, to be asked to consider it in terms of more than one theme at a time. However, it is possible, if you wish, to consider how Shakespeare draws the different themes together.

I have noted several moments when Shakespeare distances the audience from the events and likens them to a play, or to a tale. Extending that idea, we see that in *The Winter's Tale* Shakespeare has created a drama in which events grow, like a baby or a plant, from seed to maturity. In the first part of the play, it is through Leontes's jealousy that events grow, but later, we see his actions in a wider context. Time and nature are the controlling artists, under whose power the years pass and life grows, flourishes, decays, dies and renews itself. Within this ever unfolding drama, human conduct plays its part. Men and women have only partial knowledge of the drama, but they have the power to alter it for good or ill. Leontes alters it for ill. But who has the power to bring back good?

Leontes destroys life through his jealousy. Through art he can have the illusion of it again, but still and silent like death. Who has the power to set the drama of life in motion again?

The answer to both these questions could be, again, time, nature and human conduct. The reconciliation and the return of Hermione are caused by the various deeds of several characters, from the self-seeking interference of Autolycus, to Leontes's sympathy towards Florizel. Yet there remains a sense of greater wonder around three events: the truth of the oracle, the recovery of Perdita, and the preservation of Hermione. We can explain these events as being 'just a story' to be enjoyed but not believed; or as evidence of a higher power and a deeper mystery which are not fully revealed. The play suggests that there *is* a beneficient deity or force overseeing the events – pagan Apollo, the Christian God or some other power – which works through the characters in the play; a force which oversees time and nature; a force which knows, judges, forgives and redeems.

4 TECHNICAL FEATURES

4.1 LANGUAGE

When you first read Shakespeare, the difficulty of the language may stop you from understanding the meaning and experiencing the effect. The difficulty arises partly because the language is now old-fashioned, and partly because Shakespeare used language very densely, packing the words with many associations. The first task is to read the play in an edition that has clear explanations of obscure, archaic words. It may also be useful to listen to a recording of the play with the text in front of you, because the actors have already grasped the meaning (or should have!) and their delivery may help to clarify it. Some people like to see a performance, if possible, as their first experience of the play, but if you are inexperienced at listening to Shakespeare there is a danger it could pass you by like foreign film without subtitles.

Once you have grasped the basic meaning, you can begin to discover that Shakespeare's works can be appreciated both in the theatre and through study. Each play is designed to have its full meaning and effect in theatrical performance, and yet, when we sit in the theatre, the play goes by so swiftly that we are often unaware of the richness of the writing. Studying Shakespeare's language, far from spoiling its effect in the theatre, makes us more able to appreciate it to the full. One of the pleasures of Shakespeare is that we can experience his most familiar works as if for the first time. The final scene of *The Winter's Tale*, for example, has greater impact, rather than less, as one comes to know the whole play better.

The Winter's Tale, like all Shakespeare's plays, is a mixture of blank verse and prose. Blank verse consists of unrhymed lines, usually with five strong beats. It is close to natural speech, but the regularity gives the language a firm rhythm, like music with a beat to it, and that heightens the effect of the speech. But if you listened to music that went 'oom pah

pah' throughout, it would be very dull. Similarly, in blank verse, the full effect is made by what is done to vary the regularity, especially in the last plays, in which Shakespeare's use of blank verse became freer than in this earlier work.

For the scenes which Shakespeare does not wish to be so intense, or so formal, he uses prose. Often the common people speak prose while the royal families speak verse. But there are exceptions to this which you might like to examine. For example, note the prose scene between Polixenes and Camillo which brings an air of informality to the Bohemian Court (see the Commentary on IV. ii, page 26).

Some of Leontes's part in Acts I-III is difficult to read, speak or listen to because the language is so contorted. Do not be put off by this: it is part of the expression of Leontes's delusion that his speech becomes thick, his meaning muddy. Compare, for example, Leontes's speech I.ii.266-77 with that of Perdita IV.iv.117-29. Both characters are so full of feeling that it is hard to follow their meaning, but the sounds and individual words express the different nature of their passions vividly.

The sound of individual vowels and consonants can strengthen meaning. For example, in I.ii, when Camillo wishes to convince Polixenes of Leontes's fixed purpose, he keeps repeating the sounds 'f' and 'b' which lend force to his words:

> You may as well
> Forbid the sea for to obey the moon
> As or by oath remove or counsel shake
> The fabric of his folly whose foundation
> Is piled upon his faith. (I.ii.425-9)

Another variation to look for is the length of sentences. As in real life, characters often use long sentences when they are carried away by an idea, as in Florizel's passionate vows IV.iv.493-8, and shorter ones to be more decisive, as in Paulina's speech when the statue is brought to life, V.iii.97-107. In these ten lines there are no less than seventeen commands.

The more you can *hear* Shakespeare's lines the more vividly does the drama come through. If you can analyse them, all the better for study purposes, but this is not necessary to receive the pleasure of Shakespeare's dramatic use of language.

What of the meaning of the speeches? However much or little you learn from the sound of Shakespeare's language, the fundamental use of dramatic language is to communicate meaning. Characters are either conversing with each other, to themselves, or to the audience, with some aim in view. In the Commentary I have tried to show how each scene, each encounter, moves the action along either by propelling the dramatic action, or by informing the audience, or by both. Now let us look at the *interweaving* of ideas and the *double meanings* conveyed in the language and imagery.

In all Shakespeare's works, he uses language not only to communicate the immediate situation, but to convey possibilities not actualised on the stage at that moment. At the end of the Commentary on each scene I have drawn attention to the ideas introduced there which have no direct bearing on the action of that scene, or which have an additional significance beyond the present event. We noted, for example, the double meaning of the word 'issue' at many points in the play, drawing a parallel between the birth and growth of an event, and the birth and growth of a child. These ideas and images are not purely decorative, making the poetry more eloquent, they are part of the play's fabric, creating a pattern of meaning. The patterns examined in the Commentary include:

(1) pastoral imagery in the court scenes, e.g. I.ii.
(2) disease and medicine, e.g. I.ii; II.iii.
(3) sleep, death, dreams and waking, e.g. III.ii.
(4) life as a play, e.g. I.ii; III.ii; IV.iv.
(5) 'issue' meaning both the birth and growth of an event, and the birth and growth of a child.

The idea of growth is carried also in the way images *develop* through the play. We have noted several instances of Shakespeare introducing a word image which later grows into action, for example 'prison' (I.ii), 'advocate' (II.ii), 'storm perpetual' (III.ii).

One illustration of the number of meanings Shakespeare packs into one word, comes from Time's speech in which he says that he 'makes and *unfolds* error' (IV.i.2). The word 'unfolds' has a rich significance: it means that Time *reveals* error, both in the sense of (a) unwrapping what is hidden (as Perdita has been unwrapped, although her secret is not yet disclosed) and (b) telling about it, i.e. unfolding a story (the whole play tells the story of an error). It could also mean that Time can smoothe out error (as it will Leontes's by the end of the play).

You may be startled at discovering how much can be read into one word, thinking either that too much is being made of it, or that the task of understanding Shakespeare is impossibly large. Shakespeare himself may not have been conscious of the full significance of every word he used, but it is clear that as he wrote associations formed in his imagination which found their way to the page. These associations can illuminate and unify the play, and like a thread in a rich tapestry, tracing *one* through may take you through all parts of the play. Do not underestimate Shakespeare's richness. As you pursue your study of the play you will find which images and motifs help *you* to see the play as a whole, with all its layers of meaning.

If there was not such abundance in his plays, they would not have lasted through so many different periods of artistic taste.

4.2 PLOT AND STRUCTURE

Shakespeare took the story for *The Winter's Tale* from a romance called *Pandosto: The Triumph of Time* by Robert Greene. It is printed in the Arden Edition of the play. The most important changes Shakespeare made were:

(1) To create the additional characters of Mamillius, Paulina, the clown and Autolycus.

(2) To alter the ending: in Green's story Bellaria (Hermione) remains dead and Pandosto (Leontes) commits suicide.

These changes take the play to further extremes of sorrow and joy than in Greene's story. Leontes's evil is greater, including the death of his son, and it takes up nearly half the play. The joy at the end is greater, with Hermione restored to life, rather than Leontes dying.

The play is built around these very strong *contrasts*. In summary, Leontes's jealousy and its effects dominate Acts I–III. When he goes off with Paulina to repent at the end of III.ii, the action appears to have reached a tragic conclusion. The next three scenes (III.iii, IV.i and ii) are transitional, marking the important turning points from which the action opens out to comedy. Acts IV.iii and iv, and V.i and ii show happiness, then the threat to it, and then a joyful conclusion. Act V.iii shows a more complete resolution in a scene that transcends tragedy and comedy.

Throughout the play, however, Shakespeare has drawn many *parallels* through action and character. There is much *interweaving* of characters, whose appearances are distributed through the play with varied frequency. This interweaving is also of themes and images which we associate with one part of the play, but which occur in other parts too (see section 4.1).

Shakespeare has also given much attention to the way in which the story is gradually unfolded in its entirety, through a mixture of drama and report, that is, *direct action* and *indirect action*. Often the action is controlled by one of the characters, either through their *manipulation of events* (for example, Leontes III.ii (see pages 18–19); Autolycus IV.iii (see page 27); Camillo IV.iv and vi (see pages 35, 38); Paulina V.iii (see page 43) or through their narration. Shakespeare has introduced a narrator figure, Time, who manipulates events to the extent of jumping sixteen years.

One of the main tasks of a playwright is to present the whole story in the available playing time in the theatre. In some plays (notably *The*

Tempest, which he wrote soon after *The Winter's Tale*) Shakespeare structures the dramatic action and the story in parallel, that is, the time covered by the action is not much more than the duration of the play. Here, though, he condenses and stretches time very freely. The beginning of Leontes's jealousy is very sudden, accelerates quickly and takes its effect swiftly and catastrophically, with only III.i giving some slight pause. The first three Acts take place over about twenty-four days. Does the time seem more or less than that? Then comes the leap of sixteen years, followed by the long fourth Act, during which the events unravel continuously, with many smaller changes of pace and tension, through to V.i. In Act V.ii action is narrated while in V.iii the action very powerfully parallels real time.

One of the things that distinguishes theatre from film and television is that the audience and the actors are in the same real time and place. In moments when the audience is directly addressed, we are conscious of that shared time, as well as the fictional time of the drama. In Act IV.i 'Time' breaks the fictional time altogether for a few moments, but there are many other moments when the sharing of time is more important than the distant 'once upon a time' of the fiction. The last scene is, I believe, one of those moments, the audience and the characters being bound together, waiting for the statue to move.

Another way in which Shakespeare manipulates the audience is through the amount of information he conveys. It is important to be aware, throughout the play, of how much truth is known (a) to each character, and (b) to the audience. During the first three Acts the audience is as much in suspense as the characters about what Leontes will do next; after the shepherd finds the baby the audience has greater knowledge and can predict events; the 'mystery' of the final scene, though, is also mysterious to the audience. This handling of characters' and audience's differing levels of understanding leads to moments of *dramatic irony* when the full significance of a speech or action is not understood by the characters. Such moments are frequent around Perdita while her identity is known only to the audience. There are also many *double meanings* (see section 4.1) and foreshadowings of later events.

There are various ways in which the structure of the play, as outlined here, connects closely with some of its themes. Two of these themes are:

(1)   The passing of time.
(2)   Knowledge and understanding of events.

In other words, how Shakespeare presents the passing of time tells us something of what the play is saying about the nature of time. And the different amounts of knowledge and understanding which characters and audience possess, are variations on the *theme* of knowledge and belief which Shakespeare is examining.

4.3 CHARACTERISATION

In considering dramatic characters you must look at their function in the play as a whole, and at their individual qualities. It is important to consider:

(1) How far they are necessary to the plot and its meaning – do they advance the plot? Represent a theme? Show a particular viewpoint?

(2) What their main characteristics are – how do they relate to other characters? Do they develop? Why do they behave as they do?

The last point relates to *motivation*. In modern society we question *why* people or characters behave as they do, far more than was done in Shakespeare's time. His contemporaries did not always seek to discover and reveal the motivation of their characters, or even to make them develop consistently. Mediaeval drama, from which Shakespeare's developed, often used characters to personify abstract qualities, such as beauty, knowledge, the seven deadly sins, etc. The main function of these dramatic characters was to bring out the moral of the play. Too much study of the characters' psychology may lead us away from the dramatic point of a scene. Nevertheless it was one of the marks of Shakespeare's genius that he *did* draw characters whose motivations and psychological traits were more consistent and plausible than those of his contemporaries. You should pursue such analysis only insofar as it illuminates the play as a whole. Note Camillo's advice to Polixenes about not seeking to know too much about Leontes's jealousy (I.ii.431-2).

From the synopsis we see that the essential characters in the story consist of *two generations of two royal families*, plus Perdita's supposed father:

| Polixenes | | Leontes | = | Hermione |
| Florizel | = | Perdita | | Mamillius |

There is much emphasis in the play on children being 'copies' of their parents. Since the play alludes to the older generation's memories of childhood, and the younger generation grows up, there are many parallels between them which you could usefully list, with a reference to any point in the play when that parallel is brought out.

The next most important characters are the *three servants:* Camillo, Paulina and Antigonus, who contribute significantly to the working-out of the story, even though they have less to gain or lose than have the royal characters. Together, these three offer variations on the themes of honesty, loyalty, service and obedience.

When the play shifts location to Bohemia, three new characters are introduced: the old shepherd, the clown and Autolycus. They are all *comic* characters, who contribute to the lightening of tone in the second part of the play.

Finally there are the *minor characters* whose main function (apart from whatever brief part they play in the plot) is to convey the atmosphere of the scenes they appear in. For example, the courtiers in Acts I–III contribute to the formality of Court life, centred on Leontes's wishes; the mariner in III.iii contributes to the stormy atmosphere and the sense of foreboding; and Mopsa and Dorcas, together with the other servants, shepherds and shepherdesses, contribute to the atmosphere of the sheep-shearing feast.

The following notes on individual characters provide some pointers to the chief function and characteristics. The scenes noted are the ones in which the characters appear.

Leontes (I.ii; II.i; II.iii; III.ii; V.i; V.iii)

Leontes is the instigator of the evil in the play. His jealousy, remorse and penitence are traced in the Commentary, together with some aspects of his relationships. Leontes is a king, but he functions as a husband, friend and father rather than as a ruler. He uses his power as king to tyrannise publicly those involved in the affairs of his private life. Although the effect of the play does not depend on our knowing why he became jealous, Shakespeare has in fact created a fascinating case-study of pathological jealousy, delusion and slow cure. There may be some clues in Polixenes's description of their childhood (see Polixenes). We may note that, like Polixenes, he has some ambiguities in his relationships with and attitude to women: his love and hatred of Hermione are very close. He moves from passionate hatred and revulsion against Paulina to grateful acceptance of her remonstrations. He allows himself to be dominated by her, he admires Perdita as a goddess, he worships the statue: perhaps he likes women to be perfect enough to deserve his submission to them.

Hermione (I.ii; II.i; III.ii: V.iii)

Hermione is the victim of Leontes's tyranny, who overcomes death and therefore becomes his saviour. Hermione, too, is a wife and mother rather than a ruler. The fact that she is a queen increases the indignity inflicted on her and the dignity with which she receives it. Her character should be examined for warmth, eloquence, courage and patience. The central question of why she revealed herself after a delay of sixteen years must remain a mystery which may be larger than simply discovering her personal motivation. It relates to the central meaning of the whole play, whatever you take that to be (see Chapter 3). Perhaps she feels that Leontes's extreme case requires that he work out his own repentance and regain his spiritual health without her assistance. Perhaps the oracle has the answer and she submits to that, patiently waiting for its fulfilment.

Polixenes (I.ii; IV.ii; IV.iv; V.iii)

Polixenes has two functions: as the man wronged by Leontes and as the dominant father whose anger at his son leads indirectly to the reconciliation. As the third person in the triangle of suspected infidelity, he is a strangely enigmatic character. We do not see his relationship with his own queen, or much of his adult relationship with Leontes. His revulsion against the situation in Sicilia makes him leave precipitately and return only in pursuit of his son. The only women we see him with are Hermione, whose persuasions win his agreement to stay in Sicilia, and Perdita, who first charms him, then arouses his violent anger. Florizel, too, arouses anger beyond rational disapproval. The clue to his character may lie in the dialogue with Hermione in I.ii.69–85 in which, as she points out, he comes near to accusing her and his own queen of being devils, simply because they are attractive women. He is charmed by both Hermione and Perdita, but he also seems to resent the temptation women present. In each case, their charm threatens his relationship with a man, first Leontes, then Florizel.

Mamillius (I.ii; II.i)

Mamillius is the young prince who symbolises for Leontes both his own past as an innocent child and his future, through the continuity of the generations. In character he is not a total innocent but a precocious child ready to fight, tease and tell spooky stories. Leontes both uses and abuses him in the marital upset. His illness over it seems plausible, though it is difficult for us to accept that it leads to a swift death. From then on he is the 'boy eternal' existing in the mind as part of Leontes's remorse, but baulked of the chance to develop his own reality.

Perdita (IV.iv; V.i; V.iii)

Before the actress's part begins Perdita has already made her appearance in II.iii and III.iii as a baby, and may even be perceived in Hermione's appearance in I.ii and II.i. She provides the continuity of the story, the baby lost through Leontes's evil and found again, grown up, to give joy to the present and hope to the future. When she is a baby, Perdita represents innocence, which Paulina tries to use as a plea on behalf of Hermione. In the Bohemian desert she represents the secret known only to the audience, the hope that the story will end happily. When she finally appears as a lovely young woman she is the perfect mingling of princess and shepherdess, beloved of Florizel, admired by Polixenes at first, and by Camillo, who calls her 'The queen of curds and cream' (IV.iv.160). In keeping with the idea of a natural social order Perdita's true birthright manifests itself in the special qualities that have already made her 'a daughter of most rare note' (IV.ii.45). Polixenes admits that she 'smacks of something greater than herself,/Too noble for this place.' (IV.iv.158-9). In V.i her double identity is shown in another aspect: she is both a true princess and a false one. In V.iii the images finally come together and she is a princess twice over.

Many of Perdita's qualities as a young woman are conveyed through the admiration of other characters, but her development in IV.iv can also be examined through her own speeches and actions. She moves from modesty and timidity to boldness and courage in several stages which can be traced throughout the scene. She starts off very conscious that she is 'pranked up' (10) in her festival clothes and apprehensive about Florizel's royal position compared with her humble origins. She gains boldness from (a) her father's urging, (b) the role of queen she's being asked to play, and (c) Florizel's love. In the flower ceremony she expressed her opinions fearlessly, stressing the virtue of naturalness. When she realises those words were spoken to a king, who has now insulted her, she recognises that she is *not* less than him in the eyes of heaven (448-52). Much later in the scene she surprises Camillo with her firm opinion that 'affliction' does not alter true feelings (581-3).

Thus, Shakespeare has sketched in Perdita a woman who is unassuming and modest in action, but who has an unusually firm belief in the strength and worth of sincere, natural feelings.

Florizel (IV.iv; V.i; V.iii)

Florizel represents youth, love and constancy. His passionate commitment to Perdita, despite his father's anger, leads towards the final reconciliation. To Polixenes and Leontes he represents memories of *their* youth, but unlike Mamillius he has the chance to create his own present reality, beyond being a 'copy' of his father.

His motivating passion is his love for Perdita. In IV.iv this love transforms the pastoral scene from a pleasant romp amongst shepherds and shepherd-esses to a vision of eternal beauty for which he would sacrifice the universe. His passion lies behind his exaggerated claims for love, his cavalier brushing aside of his father, his decision to sacrifice his inheritance, his testing and accepting of Camillo's plan and his honest confession and plea to Leontes when the plan goes wrong.

Florizel's purpose is as unswerving as Leontes's. We shall never see if this love survives in its present form, or becomes warped or stale, as time passes and Perdita grows old.

Camillo (I.i; I.ii; IV.ii; IV.iv; V.iii)

Camillo is the servant whose loyalty is split between three masters. Camillo's role is characterised by the decision he makes in each of his three main scenes. He is a loyal and efficient servant, clear-sighted and quick to see opportunities, with a grasp of practical detail. But his loyalty, his sense of what is right and his own desires are put into conflict. His first loyalty is to Leontes, and his desire is to serve him faithfully, obediently and honestly. He is the first to hear of Leontes's jealousy. He tries to hear Leontes sympathetically, but his faith in Hermione forces him to discredit Leontes's words. In his decision to betray Leontes's confidence to Polixenes he is obeying his conscience rather than his master, and saving himself from either committing murder or being killed for not committing it; in saving Polixenes he provides himself with an opportunity to escape and serve a grateful king.

In IV.ii he chooses to stay with Polixenes and help investigate Florizel's affairs, rather than pursue his intention to obey Leontes's summons to Sicilia. He cannot know that the two matters will come together. He does not give reasons for his decision, but it does involve immediate action, which characterises his other decisions. In IV.iv his loyalty is split again, when Polixenes, like Leontes, becomes tyrannical. He stays behind to advise Florizel, and within a few minutes finds an opportunity to bring all his loyalties and desires together in a practical scheme. His skilful manipulation of the plot leads him to a double dishonesty, to Polixenes and to Florizel, but in the event, two wrongs *do* make a right. By V.i everyone understands he has been instrumental in bringing the families together. The match between Paulina and him appropriately brings together the two characters whose function has been 'medicinal' and who have 'preserved' the families, one by constantly urging the action forward, the other by keeping the past alive. Their marriage symbolises the need to look both back *and* forward.

Camillo is essentially a pragmatist, making his decisions within the immediate circumstances according to the demands he feels at that moment and the plans he can dream up to answer them.

Antigonus (II.i; II.iii; III.iii)

Antigonus is a victim of Leontes in two ways: he loses not only his life but also his honour, by being forced to perform a deed he abhors and which is against his nature. He is the only character other than Leontes who comes to believe Hermione is guilty. Like Camillo he tries at first to convince Leontes of her innocence. Failing that, the best he can achieve is the abandonment of the baby, rather than its burning. His obedience is greater than Camillo's for despite his natural kindness and tender heart he carries out the deed as ordered, modifying it only in obedience to his vision of Hermione. But he does not live to see his deed come to good.

Antigonus and Paulina are the only other married couple in the play besides Hermione and Leontes, but we see little of their relationship. They are together in II.iii, but both are entirely focused at that moment on Leontes and the baby Perdita. There is talk of their children and Antigonus hints at Paulina's quickness of tongue at home. Their domestic life is subsumed in their loyal service to Leontes and Hermione, though each expresses it differently.

Antigonus's death occurs in a confusion of storm, shipwreck and pursuit by the bear. The plot demands that he should disappear without trace, but the death itself lacks dignity and epitaph. He is a victim of the moral chaos, dying without knowing whether he has offended the 'gods' or not.

Paulina (II.ii; II.iii; III.ii; V.i; V.iii)

Paulina's role is surrounded with mystery from her first entrance to her last great deed in summoning the statue into life. She is an interfering, bossy woman who nevertheless makes herself indispensable to Leontes and Hermione.

When she comes to the prison gates in II.ii to see Hermione she is a stranger to the audience. The gaoler greets her as 'worthy lady' and Emilia accepts her plan, but she is not officially one of Hermione's ladies. In II.iii Leontes says he had expressly forbidden her to come (II.iii.42). Her audacity is well known, but she has no official function in the Court. This actually frees her to do the job she elects for herself, first as go-between and advocate from Hermione to Leontes, then as a kind of mother confessor to Leontes. Our understanding of Paulina depends on knowledge we do not at any point possess. Does she truly think Hermione is dead in III.ii? When she sees Leontes's remorse is she truly sorry she has upbraided him so bitterly (218)? These questions are carried forward to V.i when we try to reconstruct her role during the intervening sixteen years. Between Hermione, Paulina and Leontes, who is running whom? Is Paulina controlling both their lives? Or is she carrying out their wishes, caring for Hermione until the queen herself agrees to emerge, if and when the oracle is fulfilled? And helping Leontes to carry out the vow he made at the end of III.ii? Leontes's role seems very submissive, so it seems that she is the dominant one in that relationship. But the relationship with Hermione is more secret. Hermione's decision to preserve herself because of the oracle is confusingly linked with a statement that she heard it from Paulina. We do not know where the idea of the statue came from or how the whole ceremony of its unveiling was designed, and its coming to life.

Sometimes Paulina's eloquence and boldness seem admirable qualities; at other times her scolding and harping on the past may seem too much for the audience as well as some of the characters. Perhaps, without having Antigonus to nag at, she enjoys dominating Leontes and fears being displaced by some new wife; or perhaps she is entirely motivated by piety and an enlightened love for Leontes which makes her strive constantly for his salvation through repentance. Certainly, after sixteen years, she has brought Leontes to a full, penitent understanding of his own deeds, making him ready to re-enter human affairs, and receive back his wife with a free heart when the oracle is fulfilled.

Autolycus (IV.iii; IV.iv; V.ii)

Autolycus, an invention of Shakespeare's, is important from the very fact that he doesn't fit in. He was a servant of Florizel's and therefore should belong to the group of courtiers already discussed. But he has left that service and now wanders around the countryside in rags. In fact, his first function in the play is to introduce the pastoral scenes. In all his scenes he parodies the values of the other characters, giving the audience a comic and refreshing new perspective on them, in keeping with the refreshing effect of his first entrance with its song of sunshine and spring. The contrast with Leontes shifts our perspective on evil (see page 28). Other values he parodies are loyalty, constancy, honesty, courage and pride. His honesty is as refreshing and amusing as his songs. All his tricks are cancelled out by his candour in telling them. Openly confessing self-interest, he undercuts any condemnation, inviting the audience to contemplate human affairs without any moral or social code.

Shepherd (III.iii; IV.iv; V.ii)

The old shepherd is Perdita's good fortune. He finds her, rescues her and 'preserves' her and her secret for sixteen years. In creating the gullible clown, who is a more ridiculous character than his father, Shakespeare was free to make the shepherd an endearing mixture of comic countryman and dignified old man. Like the clown, he is unaware that he possesses many of the attributes of a true 'gentleman' – kindness, hospitality, a sense of his own honour. He is frank and open to his stranger guest, the disguised Polixenes, horrified at what he sees as Perdita's betrayal, completely accepting the incompatibility of a match between his daughter and the prince. Like Hermione, he is prepared for death, rather than to live without honour. He seeks Polixenes afterwards without any suspicion that Perdita might turn out to have noble origins, simply to clear himself of any part in the offence. He represents the healthy, well-balanced aspect of the pastoral life, where youth grows to old age without resentment, where a bastard child is taken up 'for pity' and where the only sins are ignorance and superstition.

Clown (III.iii; IV.iii; IV.iv; V.ii)

The clown is characterised by his comic gullibility, his simple-mindedness and his good intentions. Shakespeare makes sport of his limited experience and intelligence in his confused description of the shipwreck and Antigonus's death, his attempts to sort out his accounts and his shopping list, and the ease with which Autolycus tricks him. But he throws himself into the fun of the sheep-shearing feast, adding to everyone else's enjoyment; he is unselfish in giving money to the 'robbed' man, Autolycus; would buy trinkets for Mopsa and Dorcas if he could and is determined to help his heartbroken father after Polixenes's anger has destroyed him. His naivety about the court and courtly behaviour is comic but through it Shakespeare is able gently to satirise values which label a 'gentleman' by his outward manner rather than his inner qualities.

4.4 STAGECRAFT

The text of *The Winter's Tale* tells far more than just what words are to be spoken. If you visualise the stage (see pages 3-4) and imagine hearing the sound effects, your understanding of the play will be much enhanced.

To begin with, consider as you read *who* is on stage. Entrances and exits are the main stage directions added. They allow us to envisage the scene clearly, to be aware who is listening, as well as who is speaking, to imagine reactions as well as actions. The scenery is changed only minimally, the changes in location usually being marked by the exit of one group or individual, as the next characters enter. But there is great variety. Shakespeare has shown *public* and *private* scenes; brief solitary scenes; scenes with two characters or small groups; scenes where more than one action is going on; scenes where there is much coming and going; scenes where the action is slow or static. Find examples for each of them. Imagine seeing the play without hearing it. How much of the story would you be able to follow? Remembering how we have distinguished between direct and reported action, we realised that we *see* most of the events but *hear* about others.

Another aspect of Shakespeare's stagecraft in this play is the contrast between *movement* and *stillness*. Of course, any play is likely to combine them, but in *The Winter's Tale* some of the moments of stillness are very arresting, particularly around the mother and daughter figures of Hermione and Perdita. Hermione stands still and isolated in the trial scene, with everyone looking at her. Perdita as a baby is twice left lying helpless on the stage, first in the scene when Paulina lays her on the floor in front of Leontes, then when Antigonus lays her on the shore. On both these occasions she can do nothing for herself and the audience waits in suspense to see what will become of her. In the pastoral scene, she stands giving out the flowers while Florizel praises her. The image that she presents to him is so beautiful that he wishes she could stay like that for ever (see Commentary, page 31). The comparison to a wave is interesting because a wave is both still *and* moving as it passes, keeping its shape, but approaching the shore. These earlier moments of stillness prepare the audience to appreciate the full drama of the moment when everyone, audience and characters alike, waits breathlessly for the statue of Hermione to come to life at the end of the play, and it does.

Linking with these moments of stillness and expectation of movement, are the *ceremonial* qualities in the play. A ceremony is a sequence of prescribed actions in which all the participants are united for a common goal. The trial scene is one such ceremony, with its formal accusation, prosecution and defence of Hermione, in the pursuit of justice. However, it is an empty ceremony, because it is not in pursuit of *true* justice. Cleomenes and Dion describe the ceremony of consulting the oracle (III.i) with its priests and sacrificial offering, but we do not see it. Dances, of which there are two in the play, are ceremonial by definition, being formal patterns of movement. Here they are performed for pleasure, but many country dances were originally part of a primitive ritual performed for the good of the tribe, for example as a prayer for good crops, and some of that quality may still have been felt in Shakespeare's time. There is some ceremony, too, in the two opening scenes of the play, which are concerned with hospitality. Hosts and guests go through speeches of gratitude, welcome and mutual compliments that make up an accepted code. It may be that there is some rivalry and empty formality in these gestures, anticipating the break between the two kings. The public betrothal of Florizel and Perdita is ceremonial, with the shepherd formally joining their hands, about to pronounce their union. Finally, Paulina's formal warnings and commands make the statue scene like a religious ritual. We may note that this moment and the dances both have *music* to enhance their ceremonial quality.

The use of *costume* defines the characters in any play. Here there are also important moments when the characters adopt a *disguise*. The main function of costume in the play is to define social position: royalty, Court and country. In Shakespeare's time the difference in dress between nobility and common people was very great. This contrast is more important than the establishment of a definite historical period and geographical location for the story. In Shakespeare's time actors wore 'modern' dress with some additions. Audiences were not worried by anachronisms. For example, the worship of Apollo and the Greek or Latin names given to many of the characters suggest that the play is set in pre-Christian times but the artist mentioned in V.ii, Julio Romano, was a real painter who died in

1546. In the modern theatre it is more difficult for a designer or director to decide how to costume the characters. They might wear today's modern clothes; or the Jacobean dress worn in Shakespeare's time; or pre-Christian costumes appropriate to the story; or costumes of some other time and place that seem to bring out the meaning and effect most clearly. Consider what kind of costumes *you* would choose to help the audience understand and enjoy the play.

Once the royalty, court and country people have been established, Shakespeare introduces in the fourth Act characters who *change* costumes, starting with Autolycus, who enters in rags but explains that he once wore velvet, going on to Florizel, Perdita, Polixenes and Camillo, all of whom are not dressed according to their true rank. We have discussed these changes in costume in the Commentary on IV.iv, and noted that both the clown and the shepherd changed costume in V.ii. All these changes in appearance *invert the social position* of the character involved. This inversion is appropriate to a story about a shepherdess/princess and it helps to emphasise the social themes which dominate that section of the play (IV.iii–V.ii). Partly through costumes, the play questions (a) the relationship between true nobility and appearance, that is, the inner and outer quality of each character, and (b) whether social equality is possible or desirable.

4.5 STYLE

What kind of a play is *The Winter's Tale?* A play is an imitation of human action. No play can imitate every aspect of human life. The particular kind of imitation defines the style of the play. I have indicated the different kinds of plays Shakespeare wrote (see pages 4–5). I have also noted the influence of the morality plays of an earlier period (page 5) and the court masques that were fashionable at the end of his career (page 3). I have pointed out that *The Winter's Tale* combines the elements of several kinds of play. We may now pick out some of those elements.

Tragedy

Leontes is in many respects a tragic hero during the first three Acts of the play. He is a man of power and influence thwarted by something within himself which threatens his own well-being and that of all around him. Anguish of mind for the central character and unhappiness in those around him are important features of Shakespeare's tragedies (for example, *Hamlet, Macbeth, King Lear*). He examines the complex relationship between the hero's state of mind and the world in which he finds himself, in a situation of rapid deterioration and destruction, in which, eventually, the evil itself is killed off. Leontes is a study in the evil of tyranny, being both a victim and an agent of it. The 'tyranny' that jealousy exerts over Leontes leads him to 'tyrannise' his family and Court, extending his influence even beyond his own boundaries. The concentration on the heroes' states of mind makes Shakespeare's tragedies fascinating psychological studies of destructive or deluded behaviour. We call them tragic, though, only when the connection is made between the hero's moral sickness and the well-being of the community. With Leontes, that connection is made.

Comedy

Many characteristics of comedy are present in the second part of the play: love, intrigue, trickery, misunderstanding, amusing characters and situations. A special feature of Shakespearian comedy is the celebration of fertility and the vitality of life, especially as manifested in courtship and marriage (for example, *As You Like It*). He combines that with a realistic view of the difficulties involved in actually handling relationships. The relationship between Florizel and Perdita is more of a celebration than a realistic study, However, there *is* some examination of womanly and manly qualities which illuminates our understanding of sexual relationships. The question is raised about how bold a woman should be in her behaviour: the tragedy occurs because Leontes misjudges Hermione's behaviour to Polixenes; he also rages at Paulina for her audacity. The old shepherd wants Perdita to be bolder, but later Polixenes curses her for enticing Florizel. In the play as a whole the women's boldness is justified. Polixenes and Leontes are shown to be in the wrong. This examination of sexual relationships is typical of Shakespeare's comedies.

Romance

The Winter's Tale is often described as a romance, not meaning simply a love story, but rather a tale remote from everyday life, with strange, unbelievable incidents. The 'romantic' elements in the story are the discovery of the lost baby; the coming-to-life of the statue; and the return from death, all of which have been the centre of many other legends and tales as far back as the Greek myths (for example, Oedipus, Pygmalion, Alcestis). We have noted how Shakespeare many times stresses the pleasure of hearing strange tales, for example, Mamillius's story-telling, the 'pedlar's' ballads, the gentlemen telling about the reunion. I have suggested that Autolycus's villainies may be offset by the enjoyment involved in retelling them (see page 28). Shakespeare also invited the audience to experience the play as a strange tale, first by giving it that title (the world 'tale' does not feature in any other Shakespearian title), then by having some of the incidents related rather than presented.

A satisfying tale, however sad the incidents in it, ends happily, with all loose ends tied up. Shakespeare made even his tragedies hint at the restoration of order and harmony, and his comedies end with the nuptials, not with the difficulties he knew every marriage must contend with. The last plays, though, including *The Winter's Tale*, have even more emphasis on the working through to fulfilment and complete resolution.

Christian allegory and pagan myth

The Winter's Tale is a religious play in that it tells a story of human error, and divine power and knowledge. But Shakespeare has mixed Christianity, the accepted religion of his time, with Greek gods and mythology, which were popular subjects for art in the Renaissance period in which he wrote.

The story parallels the Christian story in depicting Leontes as a sinner who is granted forgiveness after repentance, and then experiences redemption and new life. Hermione is Christ-like in that she suffers, stands trial, dies and is resurrected. It is noticeable how often Hermione is linked with the word 'grace' which in Christian terms means the love and favour of God, granted without regard to merit. In this interpretation of the play Paulina has religious significance and may even be linked with the Apostle Paul.

But there are also clear parallels with the pagan myth of Persephone and her mother Demeter. Demeter brought fruits and plenty to the earth, but when her daughter Persephone was stolen by Pluto and taken to his underworld, Hades, she imposed barrenness on the earth. Then Pluto allowed Persephone to return once a year, and the earth flowered again. Hermione may represent Demeter, withholding her regenerative powers until her daughter is returned. Perdita (who herself alludes to Proserpina, another name for Persephone - see IV.iv) may represent Persephone who brings 'spring' to the world. This interpretation gives special significance to the 'winter' of the title, and to the many associations between Perdita and the spring.

Shakespeare's introduction of Christian and pagan ideas increases enjoyment for an educated audience as well as giving the play special meaning. The story and the characters are interesting in themselves, but an audience who can understand the richness of associations in *The Winter's Tale* will appreciate it more fully.

The main stylistic feature of *The Winter's Tale* is the *mixture* of all these elements. Tragedy and comedy are linked through the romantic story which allows happiness to be fully restored even after so much death and loss. Romance and realism are linked through the characters, who are psychologically convincing even in extraordinary circumstances. Realism and idealism run alongside each other in the pastoral scene (see Commentary, page 32).

This mixed style, shared by several of Shakespeare's last plays, has often made the play elusive to audiences, readers, critics and theatre practitioners. In Shakespeare's time consistency was not considered an important requirement. Whether or not he has bound the different elements together to make a satisfying work, has been and remains a matter for argument.

5 CRITICAL RECEPTION
AND
STAGE HISTORY

The Winter's Tale was well received during Shakespeare's lifetime and was performed at the court of Charles I in 1633. After that it fell into disrepute and was not performed for over a hundred years. The main reason was that during the period following the Restoration of Charles II in 1660, critics and audiences preferred to see plays that were tightly-structured, clearly definable as tragedy or comedy, and had a plausible story-line. *The Winter's Tale* fell short in all these ways. John Dryden, writing in 1672, criticised the play for being 'grounded in impossibilities'. Alexander Pope, editing the play in 1725, considered that much of it was not even written by Shakespeare. However, in the second half of the eighteenth century its reputation improved and it came to be admired for its freshness of sentiment and character. It was revived in London in 1741 and 1742, and praised by W. Warburton, in 1747, as a 'homely and simply, though agreeable country tale'. The pastoral scenes were much admired and were sometimes performed on their own. In 1756 the great actor David Garrick rewrote the play, setting it entirely in Bohemia, renamed Bithynia. This adaptation, called 'Florizel and Perdita', was very popular and ousted the original play from the repertoire. Garrick himself played Leontes and the actress Mrs Pritchard received much acclaim as Hermione.

In the nineteenth century the theatrical possibilities of the original version were more fully recognised. John Philip Kemble revived the play at the Theatre Royal, Drury Lane in 1811, with his famous sister, Sarah Siddons, playing Hermione. The critic William Hazlitt admired her 'true monumental dignity and noble passion' and thought the play 'one of the best-acting of our author's plays'. In other important revivals of this period it became clear that the play was an excellent vehicle for acting and spectacle. William Charles Macready played Leontes several times, his most famous leading lady being Helen Faucit in 1847 and 1848. During this period scenery and staging became more elaborate. In 1856 there was a spectacular revival staged by Charles Kean, in which the settings for the Sicilian scenes were an authentic reconstruction of Syracuse in 300BC. The Bohemian scenes, still called Bithynia, were given an exotic Asian setting. 'Time' appeared in a gorgeous pageant which linked the two halves of the play. The statue scene was also elaborate, and, as usual, impressed the audiences and critics immensely. The importance of this scene meant that the play often enhanced the reputation of the actress playing Hermione more than that of the actor playing Leontes. The great Victorian actor Henry Irving, who staged many impressive Shakespearian productions at the Lyceum Theatre did *not* produce *The Winter's Tale,* though his leading lady, Ellen Terry, made her first appearance as Mamillius in Charles Kean's production, and she did play Hermione, with Herbert Beerbohm-Tree, in 1906. But during one of Irving's absences from the Lyceum, the actress Mary Anderson presented the play there in a famous production in which she combined the roles of Perdita and Hermione.

Although the nineteenth-century versions of the play were ostensibly Shakespeare's, the text was always cut extensively, partly to put more emphasis on the main characters, partly because every scene that was presented had to be given its own setting. (Mary Anderson's production had thirteen settings.) The elaborate staging, the many scene changes, combined with the slow delivery of Victorian actors, meant that the full text would have taken far too long. Much of the comedy was cut, together with short scenes, such as that with Cleomenes and Dion. But at the turn of the century, scholars and actors alike began to look back to the methods of production in Shakespeare's time. In 1912 the actor and director Harley Granville Barker presented a famous production of *The Winter's Tale* on an 'apron' stage not unlike that of Shakespearian theatres. He rejected the heavy historical realism of Victorian productions, used startling modern designs and had his actors play at a swift pace, restoring almost all the original text. This production was a landmark, encouraging critics, scholars and audiences to appreciate Shakespeare's craftsmanship in a new way.

Since Barker, critics have studied *The Winter's Tale* with great interest, giving particular attention to its structure. They have seen the play's essential unity and also placed it in the context of Shakespeare's development as a playwright. Some critics thought all Shakespeare's final plays inferior to his great tragedies. H. B. Charlton said they were 'an old man's consolation for the harshness of man's lot', but others admired the reconciliation theme that runs through them. G. Wilson Knight wrote of these last plays under the title *The Crown of Life*, analysing the life-giving theme of 'great creating nature' that runs through *The Winter's Tale*. The play has appeared regularly in the Shakespearian repertoire, though it has never been as famous or popular as the great comedies and tragedies. The most notable British revival since the Second World War was perhaps

Trevor Nunn's production at Stratford-upon-Avon in 1969, for which the permanent setting was entirely white, with much emphasis on lighting, music and sound to create mood.

The Winter's Tale is now accepted as an authentic Shakespeare text, demonstrating some of his finest characteristics. Its theatrical qualities are irresistible, especially in the last scene. While, for some, the implausible story, range of styles and unusual structure are considered weaknesses, for others, the coming-together of so many strands of romance, comedy, tragedy, myth and allegory makes *The Winter's Tale* Shakespeare's crowning achievement.

6 SPECIMEN PASSAGE

Act III, scene i 1–22

Close examination of Shakespeare's text is invaluable for revealing how he worked as a dramatist. Conversely, when you write about a selected passage, you reveal your own understanding. No two people will see exactly the same things in it.

I have chosen this short scene because at first glance it may not seem to contribute much to the play. It is only by looking carefully at it that we can uncover its full meaning and effect.

I start with a brief explanation of *when the scene occurs* and *what happens* in it. I then explain its *main significance*. This is followed by a line-by-line examination, bringing out the *dramatic situation* and then any images or themes that have special *significance to the play as a whole*. In an examination, you need to check the exact wording of the question.

Enter CLEOMENES *and* DION

CLEOMENES: The climate's delicate, the air most
    sweet,
  Fertile the isle, the temple much surpassing
  The common praise it bears.
DION: I shall report,
  For most it caught me, the celestial habits –
  Methinks I so should term them – and the
    reverence   5
  Of the grave wearers. O, the sacrifice!
  How ceremonious, solemn and unearthly
  It was i' th' offering!
CLEOMENES: But of all, the burst
  And the ear-deaf'ning voice o' th' Oracle,
  Kin to Jove's thunder, so surprised my sense   10

> That I was nothing.
> DION: If th' event o' th' journey
> Prove as successful to the Queen – O be 't so! –
> As it hath been to us rare, pleasant, speedy,
> The time is worth the use on 't.
> CLEOMENES: Great Apollo
> Turn all to th' best! These proclamations,   15
> So forcing faults upon Hermione,
> I little like.
> DION: The violent carriage of it
> Will clear or end the business. When the
>   Oracle,
> Thus by Apollo's great divine sealed up,
> Shall the contents discover, something rare   20
> Even then will rush to knowledge. Go:fresh
>   horses!
> And gracious be the issue.   [*Exeunt*]

This scene occurs between Leontes's decision to bring his wife Hermione to trial, and the trial itself. The audience has already heard that the two messengers he sent to Apollo's oracle at Delphos have landed back in Sicilia. Now we see them, pausing on the way back to court to comment on their experience and their expectation of its result.

The very fact that nothing happens in this scene is important. First, it halts, momentarily, the relentless sweep of the action unleashed by Leontes's jealousy, giving the audience (and indeed the actor playing Leontes) a brief rest period to catch breath, before pushing forward to Hermione's trial. Secondly, as with several events in this play, we hear about the oracle but we do not see it, and that gives us a sense of its power and mystery. Both these features of the scene remind us that, despite Leontes's growing tyranny, there are forces beyond him which may affect events. Visually this idea is contained in the sealed writing which they carry.

There is no attempt to locate the scene, and little differentiation between the two characters. What we get is a clear description of Delphos and the ceremony of consulting the oracle, shared between two speakers who convey a unified impression to the audience.

And what is that impression? The first lines evoke the island itself: the words 'delicate', 'sweet', and 'fertile' contrast refreshingly with the sickly, feverish atmosphere of the previous scene. Cleomenes's response to Apollo's temple conveys a sense of wonder (2-3). Dion takes up that sense, projecting himself into a future time when he will be reporting on the ritual to people who have not shared their experience. His words convey, at first haltingly, the quality of the occasion, 'celestial', 'reverence', 'grave'. Then he breaks out more spontaneously as if the power of the ritual has burst through his hesitation: 'O, the sacrifice!' (6) and then sums up its quality with more conviction than before (7-8). Cleomenes then takes up the tale, recounting for both of them the dramatic moment when the oracle spoke so thunderously that he was 'nothing' (8-11). The lack of identity in the two characters becomes understandable in the light of this description. Unlike Leontes, who in I.ii fought to retain a sense of identity at the expense of clear reasoning, these two men have not been upset by feeling they were nothing. Instead, Dion has found the journey 'rare, pleasant, speedy' (13).

In the same speech he returns to the events at Court, the reasons for their journey, and the hope they both express, that the words of the oracle will help to clear Hermione. A sense of rush and over-exertion returns. Cleomenes hopes that Apollo will 'turn' all to the best (15), a more tranquil verb than he uses of Leontes, who has been 'forcing' faults upon Hermione. Dion speaks of the 'violent carriage' of the business (17-18) which he knows is about to come to a crisis. He is confident that when the scroll is opened 'something rare/Even then will rush to knowledge' (20-1), his words conveying the feeling that only something as powerful as the thunderous oracle could halt Leontes's headlong progress against the queen. Then he summons horses and they hasten off.

Many words in the scene anticipate later developments in the play. The description of the oracle ('celestial', 'reverence', 'grave') evokes the same atmosphere of sanctity and wonder as the final scene of the play. 'Sacrifice' anticipates the deaths of Mamillius, Hermione (supposedly) and Antigonus. Jove's thunder anticipates the storm in III.iii. The last line, 'Gracious be the issue', expresses their hope for the outcome of the trial, but the word 'issue', carrying a double meaning as elsewhere in the play, reminds us of Perdita's existence. The word 'gracious' is often used in relation to Hermione, who may represent the grace of God - a gift that must be awaited and not sought. The words also apply to the oracle itself, contained in their precious scroll. Cleomenes and Dion hope those words will bring the matter to a swift conclusion, but in fact the final outcome it prophesies will be sixteen years in the waiting.

REVISION QUESTIONS

Questions about the play will be directed *either* at specific character(s), incidents or aspects of the play, in which case you will need to relate your answer to the play as a whole; *or* to more general matters, in which case you will need to illustrate your answer with appropriate examples. You need to be able to see the connections between different dramatic elements. Take some of the themes, for example, as you revise, and see how they are expressed through characters and incidents. Then consider language, style and structure as well.

Even if a question seems to invite adverse criticism of the play, give Shakespeare the benefit of the doubt unless you are absolutely sure of your ground. In general assume that the play has a consistent meaning, that everything contributes to it, and that each scene can be effective in the theatre.

Here are some questions which may help to focus your ideas:

1. 'The story of *The Winter's Tale* is wildly improbable.' Examine *three* incidents to show how Shakespeare deals with the improbable.
2. Examine the theme of childhood and maturity.
3. 'There is more to be said for the women characters than the men in *The Winter's Tale*.' Discuss.
4. Compare and contrast the scenes in Sicilia and Bohemia.
5. What is the significance of the title *The Winter's Tale?*
6. How does Shakespeare create the appropriate atmosphere for
   (a) the sheep-shearing feast
   (b) the statue scene?
7. What contribution does the chorus 'Time' make to the play?
8. How convincing is the character of Leontes as a study in jealousy?
9. Examine the theme of reconciliation.

APPENDIX: SHAKESPEARE'S THEATRE

We should speak as Muriel Bradbrook reminds us, not of the Elizabethan stage but of Elizabethan stages. Plays of Shakespeare were acted on tour, in the halls of mansions, one at least in Gray's Inn, frequently at Court, and after 1609 at the Blackfriars, a small roofed theatre for those who could afford the price. But even after his Company acquired the Blackfriars, we know of no play of his not acted (unless, rather improbably, *Troilus* is an exception) for the general public at the Globe, or before 1599 at its predecessor, The Theatre, which, since the Globe was constructed from the same timbers must have resembled it. Describing the Globe, we can claim therefore to be describing, in an acceptable sense, Shakespeare's theatre, the physical structure his plays were designed to fit. Even in the few probably written for a first performance elsewhere, adaptability to that structure would be in his mind.

For the facilities of the Globe we have evidence from the drawing of the Swan theatre (based on a sketch made by a visitor to London about 1596) which depicts the interior of another public theatre; the builder's contract for the Fortune theatre, which in certain respects (fortunately including the dimensions and position of the stage) was to copy the Globe; indications in the dramatic texts; comments, like Ben Jonson's on the throne let down from above by machinery; and eye-witness testimony to the number of spectators (in round figures, 3,000) accommodated in the auditorium.

In communicating with the audience, the actor was most favourably placed. Soliloquising at the centre of the front of the great platform, he was at the mid-point of the theatre, with no-one among the spectators more than sixty feet away from him. That platform-stage (Figs I and II) was the most important feature for performance at the Globe. It had the audience - standing in the yard (10) and seated in the galleries (9) - on three sides of it. It was 43 feet wide, and 27½ feet from front to back. Raised (?5½ feet) above the level of the yard, it had a trap-door (II.8)

SHAKESPEARE'S THEATRE

The stage and its adjuncts; the tiring-house; and the auditorium.

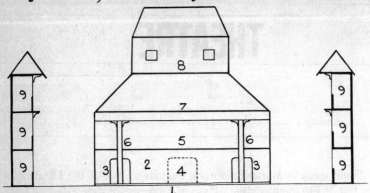

FIG I ELEVATION

1. Platform stage (approximately five feet above the ground) 2. Tiring-house
3. Tiring-house doors to stage 4. Conjectured third door 5. Tiring-house
gallery (balustrade and partitioning not shown) 6. Pillars supporting the
heavens 7. The heavens 8. The hut 9. The spectators' galleries

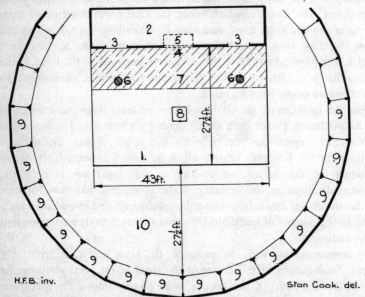

H.F.B. inv.   Stan Cook. del.

FIG II PLAN

1. Platform stage 2. Tiring-house 3. Tiring-house doors to stage
4. Conjectural third door 5. Conjectural discovery space (alternatively behind 3)
6. Pillars supporting the heavens 7. The heavens 8. Trap door 9. Spectators'
gallery 10. The yard

The Globe

giving access to the space below it. The actors, with their equipment, occupied the 'tiring house' (attiring-house: 2) immediately at the back of the stage. The stage-direction 'within' means inside the tiring-house. Along its frontage, probably from the top of the second storey, juts out the canopy or 'Heavens', carried on two large pillars rising through the platform (6, 7) and sheltering the rear part of the stage, the rest of which, like the yard, was open to the sky. If the 'hut' (1.8), housing the machinery for descents, stood, as in the Swan drawing, above the 'Heavens', that covering must have had a trap-door, so that the descents could be made through it.

Descents are one illustration of the vertical dimension the dramatist could use to supplement the playing-area of the great platform. The other opportunities are provided by the tiring-house frontage or façade. About this façade the evidence is not as complete or clear as we should like, so that Fig. I is in part conjectural. Two doors giving entry to the platform there certainly were (3). A third (4) is probable but not certain. When curtained, a door, most probably this one, would furnish what must be termed a discovery-space (11.5), not an inner stage (on which action in any depth would have been out of sight for a significant part of the audience). Usually no more than two actors were revealed (exceptionally, three), who often then moved out on to the platform. An example of this is Ferdinand and Miranda in *The Tempest* 'discovered' at chess, then seen on the platform speaking with their fathers. Similarly the gallery (1.5) was not an upper stage. It's use was not limited to the actors; sometimes it functioned as 'lords' rooms' for favoured spectators, sometimes, perhaps, as a musicians' gallery. Frequently the whole gallery would not be needed for what took place aloft: a window-stage (as in the first balcony scene in *Romeo*, even perhaps in the second) would suffice. Most probably this would be a part (at one end) of the gallery itself; or just possibly, if the gallery did not (as it does in the Swan drawing) extend the whole width of the tiring-house, a window over the left or right-hand door. As the texts show, whatever was presented aloft, or in the discovery-space, was directly related to the action on the platform, so that at no time was there left, between the audience and the action of the drama, a great bare space of platform-stage. In relating Shakespeare's drama to the physical conditions of the theatre, the primacy of that platform is never to be forgotten.

Note: The present brief account owes most to C. Walter Hodges, *The Globe Restored*; Richard Hosley in *A New Companion to Shakespeare Studies*, and in *The Revels History of English Drama*; and to articles by Hosley and Richard Southern in *Shakespeare Survey*, 12, 1959, where full discussion can be found.

HAROLD BROOKS

FURTHER READING

General background

G. B. Harrison, *Introducing Shakespeare* (Pelican, 1966).
E. M. W. Tillyard, *The Elizabethan World Picture* (Peregrine, 1963).
Judith Briggs, *This Stage Play World* (Oxford University Press, 1983).

Texts of *The Winter's Tale*

Christopher Parry, ed., *The Macmillan Shakespeare* (Macmillan Education, 1982).
J. H. P. Pafford, ed., *The Arden Edition* (Methuen, 1976).
Ernest Schanzer, ed., *The New Penguin Shakespeare* (Penguin Books, 1977).

Shakespeare plays

Any other Shakespeare plays will be useful, but particularly the other late plays: *Pericles, Cymbeline* and *The Tempest*.

Criticism

When reading criticism it is advisable to read more than one piece, so that you are not over-influenced by one interpretation. On the other hand, do not read more than you can take in. The aim of studying is to understand the play for yourself, not to know half a dozen interpretations by heart. Read to clarify, stimulate and illuminate your *own* reading of the play. The most useful anthology of criticism is:
Kenneth Muir, ed., *Shakespeare: The Winter's Tale, A Casebook,* (Macmillan, 1968).

Suggestions for further reading

S. L. Bethell, *The Winter's Tale: A Study* (Staples Press, 1947).
G. Wilson Knight, *The Crown of Life: Essays in Interpretation of Shakespeare's Final Plays* (Methuen, 1943).

84

Molly Mahood, *Shakespeare's Wordplay* (Methuen, 1957).
Derek Traversi, *Shakespeare: The Last Phase* (Hollis and Carter, 1965).